GOOD DISCIPLINE, GREAT TEENS

Other parenting books by Dr. Ray Guarendi:

Back to the Family:
How to Encourage Traditional Values in Complicated Times

Discipline That Lasts a Lifetime:
The Best Gift You Can Give Your Kids

You're a Better Parent Than You Think:
A Guide to Common-Sense Parenting

Good Discipline, Great Teens

Dr. Ray Guarendi

SERVANT
BOOKS

PUBLISHED BY ST. ANTHONY MESSENGER PRESS
CINCINNATI, OHIO

Unless otherwise noted, Scripture passages have been taken from the *Revised Standard Version*, Catholic edition. Copyright 1946, 1952, 1971 by the Division of Christian Education of the National Council of the Churches of Christ in the USA. Used by permission. All rights reserved.

(Note: The editors of this volume have made minor changes in capitalization to some of the Scripture quotations herein. Please consult the original source for proper capitalization.)

Cover design by Candle Light Studios
Cover photo ©Jupiter Images
Book design by Phillips Robinette, O.F.M.

LIBRARY OF CONGRESS CATALOGING-IN-PUBLICATION DATA

Guarendi, Raymond.
  Good discipline, great teens / Ray Guarendi.
     p. cm.
  ISBN 978-0-86716-835-8 (pbk. : alk. paper) 1. Parenting—Religious aspects—Catholic Church. 2. Child rearing—Religious aspects—Catholic Church. 3. Parent and teenager—Religious aspects—Catholic Church. 4. Discipline of children—Religious aspects—Christianity. I. Title.

BX2352.G83 2007
649'.64—dc22
                              2006034013

ISBN 978-0-86716-835-8

Copyright © 2007, Ray Guarendi. All rights reserved.

Published by Servant Books, an imprint of
St. Anthony Messenger Press.
28 W. Liberty St.
Cincinnati, OH 45202
www.ServantBooks.org

Printed in the United States of America

Printed on acid-free paper.

07 08 09 10 11 12 7 6 5 4 3 2 1

To my wife, Randi, my soulmate and best friend,
who has taught me so much about family life

Contents

Introduction
xi

ONE
The Beauty of the Beast
1

TWO
We Just Don't Talk Anymore
19

THREE
More Authority = Less Discipline
43

FOUR
Respect Yourself–and Me
71

FIVE
Trouble Trademarks of the Teens
91

SIX
Give Me Liberty, or Give Me New Parents
117

SEVEN
Standing Strong
143

Index
168

Acknowledgments

Setting out to thank all who have in any way helped put together this book would create a list longer than the first chapter. You know who you are, so thank you all very much.

A few folks need to be mentioned by name. Thank you, Hannah, for all your typing of Dad's columns. You resisted the temptation to teach your siblings how to get around my discipline. Thank you, Sarah, for taking over from Hannah, as she quit typing for me just to go to college.

Thank you, Andrew, Jon, Joanna, Sammy, James, Mary, Peter and Elizabeth, for volumes of good material. If this book sells well, your mother and I will get back some of the money that paid those exorbitant grocery bills you've brought upon us. And no whining that you only got mentioned in the acknowledgments. I dedicated the last book to all of you.

Thank you, Cindy Cavnar, my editor at Servant, for nagging me so kindly and guiding me so expertly into another book.

Thank you, God, for the ability and the opportunity to do this again.

Introduction

When are you going to write a book about teenagers?" This is a question I've heard from parents for years with more than a touch of exasperation. As a father of ten children, six of them now teenagers, I understand their sense of urgency.

Indeed, the question reflects a certain level of struggle common to guiding and disciplining kids as they move through adolescence. Perhaps no other time of parenthood is so intense in its highs and lows, its frustrations and rewards, its sense of vulnerability and satisfaction.

In my work as a child psychologist, discipline questions are far and away those I receive most from parents. Their specifics change but not their essence: How can I be a stronger parent? What can I do to stay consistent? How closely do I supervise? Can I be too strict? How do I get more cooperation? more respect? a better attitude?

There is an interesting phenomenon that occurs in my office. A parent will detail a litany of difficult and unruly behavior from the teen and then close with, "But I think I'm giving you the wrong impression. Overall he's a pretty good kid."

"How's that?" I will ask.

"Well, he's not on drugs or anything like that. I guess I should be grateful. Some of my friends are having a lot worse time with their kids."

Sometimes I will ask a parent, "What kind of child do you want looking back at you at age twenty-two? What do you want to be able to say about that person? If you're relieved to say, 'We've had a fair amount of bad times, but he is finally starting to grow up,' you can probably parent like most. Most parents don't have seriously troubled kids who become seriously troubled adults.

"But if your goal is to be able to say about that twenty-two-year-old, 'I'm not objective. I am the child's mother (or father), but he is a one-in-a-hundred kid. Morals, character, maturity, compassion—he is a beautiful human being,' then you will need to be a one-in-a-hundred parent. You will love, teach and supervise well above most. You will discipline when many parents are lax. You will stand strong when many parents yield. You will teach your children standards that are exceptional. And in the end those who benefit most will be your children."

This book is aimed at helping you raise a well-disciplined, responsible, respectful human who, at age twenty-two, will be seen by others, who are more objective than you, as a truly one-in-a-hundred young adult.

ONE

The Beauty of the Beast

Every age has its own persona, and the teen years have a pretty negative one in the majority of folks' eyes. Put me in the minority. I think that teens get a bad rap. Sure, they can be argumentative, surly and unappreciative at times—some might even say these are their better qualities. The real nature of the teen beast, though, is full of life, enthusiasm, energy and laughter.

It's up to us parents to have the strength to bring out our kids' natural best and not permit the worst to rule. Then we can honestly say to the shock of others, "I really like these teen years."

The Best Is Yet to Come

Dear Dr. Ray,

I have three children, ages nine to twelve. If I hear one more time, "Enjoy them now. Soon they'll be teenagers," I think I'll scream. Are the teen years really all that unpleasant?

Bracing for What

If you polled a thousand parents, I'm sure most of them would tag the teens as the toughest parenting years, whether from personal or others' experience. If you could take the same poll a hundred years ago, I bet the numbers would look quite different, with far less parental anxiety over the teen years. What is different? Isn't fourteen years old now the same as fourteen years old then? Have kids changed that much in just a few generations?

Yes and no. From a physical standpoint, adolescence is a universal time of dramatic change. Hormones surge, bodies stretch, and kids want to be more grown-up than they are allowed or are able to be. So in that sense, yes, the average teen pushes on a parent harder than the average littler kid, sometimes with a relentlessness or obnoxiousness new to the parent's experience. That reality acknowledged, my impression, becoming stronger the longer I am a psychologist, is that modern-day teen turbulence is more cultural than developmental.

Let's again drop back a hundred years. How likely do you think you'd be to hear the average farmer at the turn of the last century lamenting, "My boy turned fourteen last week. He's getting to be more of a teenager all the time. I can't get him to help around here as much as he used to, and he just wants to hang out with his buddies. All my friends have been getting the same kind of attitudes from their teenagers. I guess I just gotta ride it out."

Modern-day teen turbulence is more cultural than developmental.

Not a likely scenario. First, *teenager* was not a word used in 1900. It's a recent description of a slice of childhood, complete with its own meaning and personality.

Second, that farmer was likely overjoyed about his son's getting older. The boy was becoming a young man, stronger and more able to cooperate in the family's welfare. The idea that "older is harder" probably didn't cross the farmer's mind much, or if it did, it was more than balanced by "older is more helpful."

Was it our hypothetical parent's rural lifestyle that caused him to feel as he did about his teen son? Wouldn't the "city folks" see it more as we do today? Again, I don't think so.

In the past few generations, the lifestyle of the typical child has evolved into a fast-paced go-go, get-get, do-do, have-have. As kids move into adolescence, what they want to try, do and possess spirals upward dramatically. This, quite simply, is a recipe for friction. The more stuff and perks a child sees as an entitlement for "growing up," the more "teenlike," if you will, he becomes if he doesn't get it. If a parent tries to control the spiral, especially more so than other parents do, the level of teen resistance, discontent and surliness rises.

Granted, this is only one different factor of many from raising kids a hundred years ago. But I'm convinced it is a very potent one, more so than most parents realize. Therefore, to better enjoy your kids as the teen years come and go, here are a few basic suggestions.

1. Give them less materially, sometimes far less, than you are able or than their peers get. Character is better shaped by less than more.

2. Never use their peers or their peers' parents as a guide to "normal" teen social freedom. The average teen with the average parents has too much freedom too early.

3. In every decision ask the question, will this help or hurt my child's moral development? Err on the safe side. Your child is far too valuable for less.

4. Brace yourself for regular resistance and questioning of your ways. To teens "out of the norm" most often means "wrong," even when you're out of the norm because you're better than the norm.

So can you expect to enjoy your teens, or will you have to wait until most of adolescence has passed to get along well? Believe it or not, keeping your standards high will not only make for great adults someday but also for more pleasant kids along the way.

He's the Nicest Boy

Dear Dr. Ray,

My thirteen-year-old son is giving me a lot of discipline trouble. But everyone else—teachers, coaches, neighbors—says he is the nicest boy. What gives?

Is It Me

Don't worry. He probably just likes them better than you. Just teasing.

First of all, my guess is that over 90 percent of kids are better behaved with others than with their parents. Indeed, aren't most people more pleasant with nonfamily than with family? It is a fact of relationships, albeit not a good one.

Second, the average kid knows his parents far better than he knows anyone else. Consequently your son knows, often by intuition, what your discipline habits are: what you will allow, how you will respond, how long you'll nag, when you'll finally wear down, what your mood is, how many times you'll negotiate, when you've "had enough." Most likely your son has formed a detailed picture of who you are, and he acts accordingly.

My guess is that over 90 percent of kids are better behaved with others than with their parents.

Third, the majority of kids feel secure in their parents' love and acceptance. So they more easily act impulsively or obnoxiously or uncooperatively with them. In short, they relax their inhibitions with those whom they love most and who love them most.

Fourth, most people—teachers excluded—make few demands of a child. Therefore, others aren't as likely to elicit much childish opposition. Good parents, however, have rules, chores, standards—you know, the stuff kids resist. So good parents have to work harder at getting a child to cooperate with them. Put another way, you provide many more opportunities for your son to be difficult.

Now, just because it's typical for kids to treat their parents worse than they treat others doesn't mean it's good or right. Often a parent will say, "Well, she gives me a lot of grief, but she's wonderful with others. I must be doing something right." Yes and no. Yes, it's great that she treats others well. It shows she is maturing and possesses a good social sense. No, it should not be consolation for a parent who is being mistreated.

Few do for a child what a loving parent does. You deserve all the respect and good treatment—and then some—that others are getting. Indeed, parents are so important that God has given them one of the commandments.

How a child treats a mother or father ultimately becomes the adult way he will treat others. In the extreme, while he may be nice to others now, in time, if he doesn't grow to respect his family, he won't be morally mature enough to treat most anybody well.

Through his demeanor with others, your son is telling you something critical: he is quite capable of self-control and good conduct. If he can act so with others, he can act so with you. This means, and here is the hardest part, that you have to alter how he perceives you.

For instance, if he knows you will nag and negotiate, you'll have to talk less and act more. If he reads you as inconsistent in discipline, you'll have to get more predictable. If he sees you as weak in resolve—well, you get the idea. In short, you will need to teach your son that you expect to be treated well, and you will back up your expectations with consequences.

In good homes, with good parents and good kids, most of the time the gap between how a child acts with his parents and how he acts with others closes with age. By the time he is seventy-four, he should be treating you pretty well. (Again, just kidding.) Nevertheless, a really good parent doesn't wait passively for the treatment gap to close. She will make it abundantly clear—with strong discipline, if necessary—that she will help a child "honor thy father and mother."

Then, when others tell you, "He's the nicest boy," you'll be able to honestly say, "I think so, too."

After All I've Been for You

Dear Dr. Ray,

My son, age sixteen, often resists my rules with the attitude "You say I'm a good kid, but it doesn't get me anywhere. I still don't have the freedom my friends have, and they give their parents a lot more trouble than I give you."

Ungrateful

Pick one:

(A) After all I've done for you, Mother, this is the thanks I get.

(B) You should be grateful I'm not as bad as all those other kids.

(C) What do you want from me? I'm not on drugs.

(D) All the chances I've had to do bad things, and I haven't done them. You could at least ease up on me.

All of the above are variants of a common adolescent theme: "I'm playing by the rules, and you're still not willing to relax the rules." Let's analyze your son's attitude piece by piece.

"You say I'm a good kid, but it doesn't get me anywhere." Of course it does. It gets you good character, morals and a safer and more stable adolescence. If the prime goal of being a good kid is to get more freedom, more perks and more goodies, then you're not yet being good for the right reasons. Besides, why give you more chances to make bad decisions and maybe lose some of that goodness?

"I still don't have the freedom my friends have." That is true. If I wanted my son to do and have what most kids do and have, I'd raise him that way. No matter how wonderful you are, my decisions are based upon your continuing welfare. I won't relax my standards simply because you've kept them. That's not good for you.

Why would I want to change the very ways that helped me raise a son like you?

"They give their parents a lot more trouble than I give you." I can't know that for sure, but I'll take your word for it. And that just proves my point. You are who you are, in part, because we are who we are as parents. Therefore, why would I want to change the very ways that helped me raise a son like you? I'm proud of you, and I want to stay that way. Your character is not measured by how you stack up to others with less character. It's measured by how you yourself act, independent of your friends' actions.

Your son is echoing a modern attitude. Coming from teens it's the "I'm not on drugs" claim. Across all ages it's the claim, "Well, I could be a lot worse. At least I'm not as bad as that guy." As cultural morals decline it becomes easier to feel satisfied that one is comparatively moral.

Continue in your high standards, and your son will most likely mature past his moral relativity and judge character by more absolute standards of right and wrong. After all, he is still a kid, and a pretty good one. He has time to become morally more clear-eyed.

A final thought. Next time your son implies that you "should be grateful," respond with, "I am grateful. It could be a lot worse. After all, I don't neglect you or mistreat you. And I'm not on drugs."

Middle Child Syndrome

Dear Dr. Ray,

I have three girls, ages ten, thirteen and fifteen. Our middle daughter can be very difficult, much more so than her sisters. Lately I've read about "middle child syndrome," and some of its features sound like hers

Middle Mom

Let's first summarize some of the main features of middle child syndrome. The middle child gets lost in the family. He doesn't have the privileges given the oldest or the attention given the youngest. He's literally caught in the middle, unsure of how he fits into the family schemata. Consequently he's prone to identity problems and misbehavior, especially to get attention, because he feels that bad attention is better than no attention.

There's only one thing wrong with this plausible-sounding description. It's false. Middle child syndrome doesn't exist. It is a media disorder, largely concocted and promulgated in the popular press. True, some middle kids do have identity or behavior problems, but so do some oldest kids, some youngest kids, some only kids and some second from the last fraternal twins.

Middle child syndrome is a media disorder, largely concocted and promulgated in the popular press.

Tongue planted firmly in cheek, I tell parents, "If you really fear middle child syndrome, don't have an odd number of kids. If you already have three or five, have another. Wipe out that middle spot. If you have seven, nine or eleven, middle child syndrome is probably the least of your worries."

In fact, the research on birth order and its effects on personality is very inconsistent and inconclusive. Rather than a child's place in the family order bringing with it certain characteristics, birth order seems to exert a negligible if any effect on a child. The only research with some consistency concerns oldest or only children. As a group they tend to be slightly more independent and achieving. And I'm not so sure how much of that is due to their position in the family.

I think we parents change our style a lot. With the first child we boil everything that comes within fifty feet of her. By the time the last child rolls around, we throw her a big dirtball and say, "Here, chew on this. And wipe your mouth off on the bushes before you come into the house."

The first child has double photos of every burp and potty visit. The last child has one picture from the hospital and one from his wedding rehearsal dinner. And when he finally notices, "How come I have no pictures, Mom?" we fudge, "No film for the camera, Honey. Besides, you look like your sister. Use her pictures."

I don't doubt that your daughter is struggling harder than her sisters to grow up, and possibly some of this may be related to that middle spot. But it is likely due primarily to something much more powerful: her temperament. The fact that she's your middle daughter may be coincidental. She very well could exhibit the same behaviors whether she was your oldest or youngest, again because of her nature or inborn personality style.

This is not to say that you won't have to deal with the "extra" troubles your daughter experiences on her way to adulthood. You will, but she doesn't have a "syndrome." She's uniquely she, and you, being her mother (Are you an only mom or a middle mom?), are in the unique position of helping her mature.

By the way, I've often wondered how long a child has to hold the middle position to develop MCS (you know a disorder has arrived when you can call it by its initials). My daughter was our middle child for two years until we adopted our son (child number four). Is MCS something she can outgrow, or will she always be a middle child at heart?

This is something my wife and I pondered as we moved our way up to being parents of ten. Over the years we had four different middle children. How long does a child have to be a middle child to contract "middle child syndrome"?

The Letter Phenomenon

Dear Dr. Ray,
What do you think about all the different diagnoses that children are labeled with these days? It seems new "disorders" are popping up constantly.

Letter Alone

Pick a child, any child. Don't raise him well. Leave out a lot of love. Drag him through adult-created chaos and turbulence. Expose him early and often to toxic media and entertainment.

Or love him lots but discipline him little. Be permissive, erratic or weak in parenting. Overindulge, give too much of everything—freedom, perks, goodies. For whatever the reason, from malignant neglect to spoiled-rotten indulgence, don't consistently, resolutely teach morals and character.

Over time the child grows, but his socialization doesn't keep pace. And depending upon his inborn temperament, he can become capable of much that is ugly: immature, nasty, violent, bizarre, inexplicable or conscienceless conduct.

Then come the questions. What's the problem here? Why is this child acting this way? Is there a psychological problem? an emotional disorder? unresolved anger? deep-seated disturbance?

Professional analysis often follows. A person like myself assesses and concludes, in essence, "Yes, I've studied this child. He does appear disordered. He has letters. He has ODD, ADD, ADHD, LSMFT, IRS, EIEIO." The letters begin to compete, all in an honest attempt to explain what's wrong with this youngster.

Don't misread me; I'm not asserting that legitimate diagnoses don't exist. What I am asserting is that, in my opinion and experience, these diagnoses are being grossly overused. They are being pinned on too many kids, too easily, too quickly. Much lies in how they are defined, as boundaries are often vague and subjective.

We adopted our son Jon when he was four. His womb life and early months were marked by drug exposure and neglect. As a toddler he was placed in foster care, where he was cared for well but disciplined seldom.

During our early visits with Jon, among other bits and pieces of misconduct, he punched me in the face, attempted to strangle my wife and kicked the foster father about ten times. His behavior was unlikable and hard to manage. In time the letters started as the attempt was made to understand Jon psychologically.

I diagnosed Behaviorally Regressive Attitudinal Trauma (BRAT).

Twelve years later none of those letters have held up except those I gave Jon when I first met him. I diagnosed Behaviorally Regressive Attitudinal Trauma (BRAT). Yes, Jon looked as if he was disturbed, but the real problem was that he'd not been socialized well.

Today Jon is showing what he really is. He is a young boy with an eager-to-please, gentle nature—a nature that had been buried for some time beneath a growing, nasty ball of ugly behavior and habits. That was his problem, not a mental disorder.

If grown-ups don't do what is needed to love, teach and discipline a child, the child can reflect the lack—although it amazes me how many children actually mature far better than they have been raised. What the child exhibits are problems, to be sure, but they are not innate to the child. In other words, the parents didn't get cursed with a demon seed that nobody short of God could raise. Far more often the child is only doing what has come naturally, given what hasn't been done to both nurture and control him.

So the proliferation of diagnoses placed upon children is in large part, I believe, a consequence of family fragmentation, moral chaos and indulgent permissiveness in various combinations. True, not all diagnoses are questionable, but a significant number, in my experience, are explained better as a function of big people-little people dynamics rather than as some internal disorder that afflicts the child.

Attention-Starved?

Dear Dr. Ray,
What do you think of the idea that kids misbehave to get attention; therefore, if a parent ignores bad behavior, it will go away? Even with teenagers?

Ignore-ant

The idea that kids misbehave to get attention is one on which I was nursed educationally. Fortunately, I didn't pay much attention to it. And now, after twenty-five years of observing parents and kids, I am even more convinced that it is mostly false.

Here's the gist of the "kids act bad to get noticed" theory:

1. Kids want attention.
2. They'll find ways to get it.
3. Bad attention is better than no attention.
4. Acting bad will force grown-ups to pay attention.
5. Discipline is the price to pay for attention.

Plausible sounding but, for the most part, faulty. Kids do want attention, and they will push for as much as they can get. It does not follow, however, that the typical motive for the typical kid's misbehavior is to force attention. Most kids, as studies suggest, misbehave for one psychologically complex reason: They want to do what they want to do. Indeed, don't we all?

Motives for misbehavior are nearly endless: impulse, frustration, control, deception, manipulation, aggression. (Sounds like the promo for an upcoming mini-series, doesn't it?) Most children quickly learn that getting attention is not a priority reason for acting up, especially if it comes in the form of discipline. Discipline carries too many negatives, particularly if parents are consistent.

It is more accurate to say that kids *can* misbehave for attention or that they *can* gain from the resultant upheaval or control or parental agitation. But these are effects, not necessarily motives.

In loving homes a lack of attention is not usually a cause of misbehavior; in fact, sometimes it's just the opposite. Attention is what's keeping the trouble rolling.

Let's say that Holmes is arguing for permission to go to Watson's house. Neither his homework nor his daily chores (Do kids still have such prehistoric things as daily chores?) have been started, much less completed. The more you debate over why he can't leave until fulfilling his responsibilities, the longer he'll debate, and the hotter the exchange will become. After twenty-seven minutes of word lock, I doubt you'll be saying, "Holmes, we've been calmly interfacing for nearly half an hour, and I must admit, I'm beginning to experience some pangs of frustration."

Your point-counterpoint is a form of attention. The argument will only subside when you stop the words by refusing further discussion or by telling Holmes that any more debate will lead to an automatic no, extra chores or an early bedtime.

Some kids are attention-seekers because they get too much to begin with.

The "misbehavior for attention" notion also heaps guilt on good parents. If Tallulah is misbehaving just to get attention, does this mean she's not getting enough from you? Is your parenthood deficient in this regard? Is her obnoxiousness really all your fault? You may be just too oblivious or self-absorbed to raise a good kid.

Nonsense. Good parents give plenty of attention. They may not give all a child wants, but what children want is not always good for them. Some kids are attention-seekers because they get too much to begin with.

Naturally it follows that if attention is not a prime motive for misbehavior, ignoring the trouble won't usually make it go away. Most misconduct has to be dealt with effectively in order to reduce it and to teach a lesson about life.

There's a pretty straightforward law of discipline: the more passive your discipline, the longer it takes to work. You may not be yielding to the demands of a temper fit as you attempt, however vainly, to tune it out, but you are also not holding Stormy accountable for the rudeness, nastiness or violence of his fit. Discipline works more quickly when a parent is willing not to ignore but to act decisively and firmly when called for.

One last logic problem: if Harmony is truly acting up to gain your attention and you don't give it, why then wouldn't she escalate her misconduct until she gets it? If ninety-decibel screaming evokes no reaction from you, why not kick it up to 110 and see what happens?

If x amount of misconduct doesn't force you to respond, why not go to $2x$ or add y?

Sometimes doesn't it seem that kids are too smart for us psychologist types and our theories? I just don't pay any attention to them.

Forced Contact

Dear Dr. Ray,

My thirteen- and fourteen-year-olds, who used to love to be with my husband and me, are more and more reluctant to go anywhere with us. They always seem to have "something better" to do. Should we force the issue?

A Twosome Again

Ah, sweet parental revenge. During the first nine or ten years of life, the kids embarrass us in public; after that we embarrass them.

"Ah, c'mon, Dad, don't wear the shirt with the feathers again."
"Mom, please don't wave to me when other people are looking."
"Just drop me off here; I'll walk the last couple miles."

During the first nine or ten years of life, the kids embarrass us in public; after that we embarrass them.

Listening to grandparents and older, I've come to believe that the great adolescent aversion to being with us dorky grown-ups is as much cultural as developmental, if not more so. In the not-so-distant past, double-digit age did not predict routine resistance to public parental contact. Only as life for kids has become more frenetic and entertaining has the competition for what used to be family time exploded.

I mean, why should Freeman want to go out to eat with his mother—a high-level treat a few generations back—when he can call friends, surf the TV, play computer games or get picked up by Harley, who has a bigger TV, 3-D video games and a cute sister who also stayed home to avoid being with her parents? In short, it's not always that your kids aren't pulled to be with you; it's that the pull to be elsewhere is much stronger. As the entertainment options expand with age, and nowadays they do so exponentially, former top-ten pick—being with Mom and Pop—drops to number forty-seven.

Many experts solemnly intone: It is normal and healthy for adolescents to separate from adults and to assert their desires in the development of independence, or some such psycho-verbiage. I'll bet their kids don't want to be with them either. Certainly some separating is natural. But how have we come to label wanting to spend little time with one's parents as healthy, psychologically speaking?

Further, just because something is natural doesn't mean it's welcome or even always good. It also doesn't mean you have to stand back passively and let it dictate family life. So what if Freeman would rather be elsewhere than with you?

What do you gain by forcing him to attend his little sister's Christmas play or to visit elderly Aunt Agatha, the lady who always cries when she sees how big he's getting and who wants to hug and kiss him good-bye and give him a dollar? I mean, how much trauma can he take?

The answer depends on what you want to teach. If you don't mind that Freeman always chooses adolescent freedom over family, then let him pursue his pursuits. Probably someday he'll pass through this phase, although in the meantime the song "Cat's in the Cradle" could make you nervous.

On the other hand, if you want to teach Freeman that, like it or not, some things are more important than entertaining himself, then at times you do need to insist he go your way instead of his. Gee, is it hard to figure in which direction I lean? You don't have to be a shrink to read between these lines.

Well, you might say, we do spend time together at home. True, but if you're like most families, even home time is at a premium. Why give teens the authority to decide to reduce further what little family time you have? More importantly, not all lessons in character are taught at home.

A visit to Aunt Mary's, however boring in modern society's measure, can teach manners, sacrifice, respect for elders and compassion.

Is all this to suggest that you hog-tie your kids and drag them kicking and screaming everywhere you go? Would you even want to do that? I don't think so. I do think, however, that you need to judge each together time on its merits and not on whether your kids want it.

Believe it or not, sometimes good times occur because parents insist on it. Once past their initial resistance, the kids find that this isn't all so bad, assuming, of course, you change that shirt and don't do anything too uncool, like snort when you laugh. And even if your children don't cooperate now, chances are they'll see it differently someday. Many young adults have told me how grateful they are for those times of forced family contact, as forever memories were made.

There's an unexpected bonus to one-sided togetherness. The kids will be so ecstatic whenever they don't have to be with you, they'll probably do just about anything to earn freedom, even be nice to you in public.

Hyper-Activitied

Dear Dr. Ray,

What do you think of the activity level of many families today, running endlessly from meeting to game to event?

The Taxi

Your question has been sitting on my desk for months. I finally got to it while sitting in the car, picking up my son from ball practice early because my daughter's skating lessons were canceled. Or was it during my youngest son's soccer game rain delay?

No doubt, families have become more hyperactive in the last few decades. The phenomenon is succinctly captured in those Christmas newsletters sent to family and friends at year's end. I suspect such updates are needed because no one saw each other much in the past twelve months of mutual busy-ness.

"Our daughter Mackenzie, now eleven, just finished her twelfth consecutive year of ballet, gymnastics, competition power-lifting and ancient Semitic language scholarship. After her 2008 Olympic tryouts, she will be seeking a Junior Ambassadorship to NATO. And little Marshall, who just turned six, earned his black belt in karate, added sax as his third instrument of choice and took first place in the National Spelling Bee. I'm trying to stay busy with…"

The activities trend is an example of pursuing the good at the cost of the best. Certainly sports, music, clubs and interests all provide positives for kids and their character. The trap for most of us lies in learning the balance between flurry and family, between pace and peace. Little League ball for six-year-olds can be fun, but not when it requires two games a week with practices on all off days.

The activities trend is an example of pursuing the good at the cost of the best.

One mother told me that upon realizing that, over a couple of years, she had been pulled into an ever-faster treadmill, she said to her two adolescent sons, "During your bath tonight, decide which two activities you wish to keep. The rest will be discontinued." It was her way of regaining some control of the flow of her family. A few weeks later the boys were no worse for lack of wear, and they were more settled.

Families need open time, lots of it. For it is in the open time that good times spontaneously happen: a giggling conversation, heading out for ice cream, sitting and teasing in the kitchen, a cutthroat game of "Go Fish." Negotiable time is the stuff of closeness.

How do you know you're pursuing the good but losing some of the best? Ask a few questions:

1. Do you have a nagging sense that your time is being gobbled up, either in the schedule of events or their juggling? Trust your instincts on this one. Cut back.

2. Do you seldom eat together as a family, as someone always has someplace to be?

3. Do your kids complain routinely about being bored? It's an irony that the more we strive to fill each minute, the more easily we become bored.

4. When is the last time you went more than two days without a scheduled activity?

5. Can you and your spouse regularly attend the kids' events together, or is each of you at a different event with a different kid?

By the way, I was just kidding about writing this column while sitting in the car. I wrote it at home, while my wife was sitting at soccer practice, just before she had to drop Sarah at her violin lesson.

TWO

We Just Don't Talk Anymore

My guess is that hundreds of books have been written on the art of communicating with teens. If only the kids would read them. Most of these books, if not all, are grounded on the same theme: Grown-ups need to learn how to talk and listen better so the kids will hear us, understand even.

The message in many of these books is not subtle: If your kids aren't getting this, obviously you're not communicating well enough. If you were, every so often you'd hear something like, "Oh, Mother, I've been so blind. Now I see what you're saying. Of course, that's why you're the parent and I'm the child. Let's hold hands and sing 'Kumbaya' around the campfire."

In any interaction with teens, by definition there's an unpredictable variable: the teen. So while we all can learn to be better at this communication thing, sometimes the best communication is knowing when to quit communicating.

Communication is most effective when *all* the parties are reasonable. Need I say more?

Somebody Speak to Me

Dear Dr. Ray,
I used to be able to talk with my kids. They're teenagers now, and I can't seem to get through to them on much of anything. Any ideas?
Talk to Me

Your question, I'm sure, has baffled billions of parents over countless generations. I can imagine fathers everywhere thousands of years ago lamenting, "These kids nowadays. All they want to do is wear shoes. I tell them, these things are a passing fad. But do they listen?"

A deaf-to-parents phase is an adolescent rite of passage. Almost all kids pass through it and emerge, for the most part, more open-minded on the other side. To paraphrase Mark Twain, "When I was fifteen, my father was the dumbest man in the world. Amazing how much smarter he got by the time I was twenty-one."

Take some consolation: it's pretty typical for your teens to see you as someone badly out of rhythm with the present world, a lost soul who's gained little knowledge of life in forty-two years.

Some of the world's brightest folks have written on the art of communicating with teens. Certainly I can't scratch the surface of this topic in our brief space. But I can share some basic don'ts and dos.

Don't lecture. Teens have a very strict definition of what constitutes a lecture. A lecture is 1) any sentence over seven words, 2) any compound sentence, 3) any group of words beginning with "When I was your age," "Now listen here," "And another thing," "Let me tell you something," or, "You know, I wasn't born yesterday."

Teens reflexively shut down in the face of a lecture. Their eyes glaze, their faces go slack, and they cease to register any incoming information except, "Do you have anything to say?" To which they reply, "No."

We parents define *lecture* much more broadly. We allow ourselves upward of fifty thousand words before we call something a lecture. The fact remains, if we want a chance of being heard, we'd best avoid one-way monologues.

Don't compare childhoods. Remember how you tuned out such recollections? Nothing's changed. Our kids believe that our childhood has no relevance to them whatsoever. Whatever point we're trying to make is lost on them because they know that all we really had to worry about was not being eaten by dinosaurs as we walked on all fours through six square miles of overgrown jungle full of snakes and spiders.

Keep your explanations in the present: "I'm not letting you go to the party because I don't think there will be enough supervision." You may not be any more understood, but at least you won't get that look that says, "Tape Number 102: I didn't date until I met your mother in my senior year...."

Don't try to discuss the problem in the heat of the moment. To adolescents *discuss* means we talk and every twelve minutes they grunt just to let us know they're still conscious. The heat of the moment, though, is the very time we feel most pressured to explode and make clear exactly how we feel about finding a pack of cigarettes in Winston's coat pocket. Of course, he says he's holding them for his girlfriend, Salem. We believe otherwise, but for the meanwhile it might be wise to let the issues rest.

For one thing, Winston knows where we stand on smoking; he's lived with us for fifteen years. For another, when all parties are calmer, there's a much better chance of clearing the air. Explosions don't clear the air; they cloud it.

Lest you now are thinking, "Dr. Ray, you have just wiped out my main communication strategies," here are a few replacement options.

Do ask questions. Understandably we feel the overpowering urge to try to straighten out immediately Oxford's wayward thinking when he tells us it's good to get Cs and Ds as a freshman so you can improve your grades later in high school and people will think you're getting smarter. Sometimes if we ask a few clarifying questions (What will colleges think? What do you think I'll do about your poor grades?), Oxford may not only tell us more of what's on his mind but also see the illogic or shortsightedness in his reasoning. That's a "maybe."

Do let some subjects ride. To illustrate, sixteen-year-old Maynard comes home with a revelation: "Mom, Roscoe's brother has a friend whose cousin's neighbor sold Christmas cards last month, and he made two thousand dollars. I could do that and just skip college."

Your first impulse might be to fire off, "Oh, so you think Christmas rolls around every month, and you can build a future selling cards?"

Try stifling this instinct for a day or so. As long as Maynard intends to keep his grades up just in case he changes heart and heads for college, it's not urgent to challenge his career choice yet. Most likely he'll sidle in three days from now with, "Mom, I changed my mind. I want to be a brain surgeon." Then you'll have to fight the urge to cry, "You think you can get into medical school with those grades?" With teens sometimes the best way to be heard is not to talk for a while.

Do plant a seed. Faith's friend isn't a friend in your opinion. She takes advantage of your daughter's trusting nature, but Faith hasn't noticed that yet. One day Faith tells you how surprised she is that Jewel has no intention of repaying her the ten dollars she borrowed.

Instead of an "I was wondering when you'd find out what she was really like," try a softer observation: "Friends need to be picked carefully," or, "Sometimes people don't act the way we thought they would," and then let the matter drop.

When the emotion hits, even adolescents want to talk, even to us parents, even if because we're the only ones around.

You've planted a seed for thought, and Faith will be more likely to mull over your quietly spoken words than a torrent of opinion. Give your seed time to take root. When Faith has thought things over, she'll probably bring up the issue again.

Do let your kids know you're always ready to listen. When the emotion hits, even adolescents want to talk, even to us parents, even if because we're the only ones around. Most things we parents are occupied with can be set aside temporarily. Take time; make time to be there.

Communicating with adolescents can sometimes be as fruitful as running headlong into a brick wall. But didn't we all have a lot of bricks in our makeup once? Most of us still have a few.

Then again, there is a risk involved in hearing what kids have to say. It may scare us to the point that we appreciate a little ignorance.

Listening Stamina

Dear Dr. Ray,

My thirteen-year-old daughter complains that I don't listen enough before giving her my opinions. How can I listen longer?

Listening

A remarkable coincidence (or maybe some farsighted linguist planned it so) is that *listen* and *silent* contain the same letters. Good listening begins with silence. The fewer words we interject while someone is voicing her thoughts, the more thoughts we'll hear.

Alas, holding our tongue is much easier to talk about than do, especially as it becomes worrisomely clear that what we're about to hear we're not about to like. Sometimes the kids are talking on impulse: "Mom, I think I'm going to move to the South Pole when I'm eighteen. The solitude will help me find myself." Sometimes they're sounding foreboding: "Dad, you may be getting a letter from school tomorrow." Sometimes their words are pure fancy: "You know, schools should offer swing shifts, like factories do. I'd get better grades on midnights."

To prolong your listening stamina, start with this thought: nothing is made worse by listening.

Whatever the gist of the message, after hearing about six words, most of us are ready to unleash a torrent of parental commentary. We're driven by the fear that if Watson's elementary reasoning continues unchallenged for more than a few minutes, it'll take root.

To prolong your listening stamina, start with this thought: nothing is made worse by listening. Even if Perry already has mapped out his itinerary to the South Pole, he hasn't left yet. There's still time to explore the full details of his excursion. Who knows, as he talks about his plans, he may raise the same questions you would. Similarly, if Stanford already has skipped the classes that generated the letter from school, he can't be skipping any more while he's standing in front of you, not unless he's incredibly creative.

In essence, as long as your daughter is talking and you're listening, nothing bad is happening. One parent said she felt fully secure only when her son was talking to her. Whatever he was saying, he wasn't out somewhere doing it.

A personal gag order is another way to listen longer. Resolve not to utter one comment or opinion for, say, one minute. Watch the clock if you have to. If one full minute of silence for you would be comparable to running a marathon race the first morning you take up jogging, gradually build up your listening stamina. Begin with twenty seconds or roughly the amount of time your daughter takes to walk into a room, look at you and say, "Mom, if I tell you something, promise you won't get mad?"

Quiet attentiveness does more than passively permit communication. Sometimes it can compel kids to talk. Our silence creates a word void they're not accustomed to, and they may feel the urge to fill that void with their own words, thus giving us a deeper look into their thoughts.

Good listening begins with silence and then moves to understanding. One father would say little until his son finished talking, whereupon Dad would paraphrase what he heard to make sure he heard it correctly. A mother preferred the "five w" approach with her ten-year-old: who, what, when, where, why. Only when she knew all five answers would mom offer an opinion or advice or mete out discipline.

There's an old saying: it is better to keep your mouth shut and let someone think you're dumb than to open it and remove all doubt. This has relevance for raising kids. The longer we listen, the more likely we are to speak with credibility and authority when we do speak.

The Quality Is in the Quantity

Dear Dr. Ray,

What is your opinion of "quality time"?

Clock-watcher

"Quality time" was conceived in the minds of experts who asserted, "It doesn't matter how much time you spend with children as long as it's good time." Just make sure that your moments with Daley are as mutually satisfying and psychologically fulfilling as possible, and you really needn't be concerned about the amount of time. In short, it's the quality not the quantity that counts.

Certainly everyone would agree that positive time with kids is better than negative time. If 61 percent of your minutes with Melody are spent in disharmony, you might be wise temporarily not to try so hard to be together. A little distance may be the very thing that improves the relationship.

All things considered, if quality time is defined as time enjoying each other's company, who could dispute that this is good? The potential for abuse lies in quality replacing quantity.

First of all, quality is a slippery entity. It resists being plugged into a timetable. The older a child, the harder it is to get her to cooperate with our schedule of quality programming. Today's teens have so many options and so much mobility that they might only be willing to book an appointment with us next Sunday night at 11:45 PM. Quantity time allows the parent to do the booking.

Second, quality time all too often means entertainment time, with our finding some activity to offer our youngster so we can "share the experience." But quality comes in many forms. When a colleague asked a grown daughter what she remembered most about her father, she said that few particular events or activities with him stood out. Rather, he just always was there for her.

While quality time conjures up the idea of interaction, some of a child's warmest, most secure moments can come from a parent's passive presence. One father said, "If the kids are playing in the family room, instead of reading my paper in the kitchen, I'll move to the family room and read there." He didn't take part in their playing; he didn't try to talk with them even; he just quietly raised his profile. It was his silent way of saying, "I'm right here, kids." Some of the highest quality parenting is born of what we don't say and how we show it.

Quantity time also leads to spontaneity. For unplanned quality to occur—a post-bedtime trip in pajamas for ice cream, a tickle fight on the couch, a late night after-date talk—it often needs quantity as a partner. The relationship is elegantly simple: the more quantity, the more quality.

Boredom has value in and of itself. It slows the pace. It sets the stage for memories woven in love.

One parent, looking back on two decades of motherhood, said, "Parents and kids nowadays need more time to be bored together." What? Seeking boredom while immersed in a culture that says, "Act, move, do, be entertained"? After twenty-five years of shrinking, I'm inclined to agree with this veteran mother. Boredom has value in and of itself. It slows the pace. It sets the stage for memories woven in love.

If common sense tells us that quantity time matters, why has the concept of quality time emerged so popular? Quality time is a natural outgrowth of a society on the run and wanting to justify itself with its children. Kids are blessedly flexible and resilient, and in the short term they will allow us to skimp on them. It is in the long run that we and they risk losing those somethings we can never get back. If our lives are stuffed full, there is much to cut back on that is far less valuable than our children.

In the end reality always wins. And the reality is that time is absolutely indispensable to high-quality parenting. Time is the framework upon which all other aspects of family are built. It takes time to consistently discipline. It takes time to catch teens in the mood to talk with us (an event on a par with Haley's Comet). It takes time to teach, hug, pray, cry, be frustrated with each other and then make up.

No matter how high the quality, it alone cannot form the bonds of a relationship. That takes quantity. It always will.

Parents Are From Venus

Dear Dr. Ray,

I try hard to understand my teenager's feelings about things, but whenever I stand my discipline ground, I hear remarks like, "You never listen," or, "You just don't understand." What am I doing wrong?

I Do Understand

Probably nothing. For a couple of generations now parents have been hammered by the experts about the dangers of being communication Neanderthals and about the "how to" magic of being psychologically savvy listeners. It's no surprise so many wonder, "What's wrong?" when their kids accuse them of being hard-hearted, hardheaded dictators.

A hundred years ago on the spot you now live most likely sat a farm. That farm mom had a 5 percent chance of having a high school education. But she could have instinctively told you, "Kids won't understand or like much of what you do as a parent. They will some-day, and that's what matters most."

Nowadays parents are made to feel incompetent—communica-tively challenged—if Sherlock doesn't understand them. Obviously they're listening passively instead of listening actively. They're using a "you message" when an "I message" is called for. Their positive-to-negative statement ratio is only three-to-one instead of the ideal seven-to-one.

Certainly parents can communicate poorly: teens can bring out the worst of interaction styles in us adults. And certainly there are plenty of ways to make a tense discipline confrontation worse. But my experience with parents, teens and discipline has taught me repeatedly that

The only foolproof way to be perceived as an awesome listener is to give your teen exactly what she wants. when a parent truly is trying to understand the child, more often than not it is the child who is being unreasonable rather than the parent.

When Holmes accuses, "You never listen to me," or Harmony whines, "Just once I wish you would see my side," I regularly find that the parent has listened quite empathetically, with heroic patience even. In the end she just didn't change her decision, and that's what brought on the recriminations.

The only foolproof way to be perceived as an awesome listener is to give your teen exactly what she wants. "You mean you'd like to go to the mall unsupervised with your friends? Of course. Now I'm hearing you." "You are asking to do your homework after 9:30 PM when you're more awake, aren't you? Why didn't you just say so?" "Let me see if I understand this. You want to borrow my car to take your five friends to the big-time wrestling matches? Well, sure. Let it never be said that I'm not an open-minded parent."

Unfortunately, the cost of avoiding the poor listener accusation— that is, giving in—is way too high a price for a parent and more so for the child. Better to listen as long as you see fit and then quietly end the discussion with, "I do understand your point, but I don't agree with it. And I must do what's best for you because I love you." (That "love line" really makes kids mad, because down deep they know you mean it.)

Active listening, to use modern psychological jargon, means hearing what another truly means. OK then, what Oral is often saying when she is saying, "You don't listen," is really, "You don't change your mind to agree with me." So next time you get charged with lack of listening, you could reflect back, "What I'm hearing you say is that

I'm not agreeing with you." So you see, even when you're "not listening," you're actually therapeutically listening.

Tricky stuff, this psychology.

With Respect to Feelings

Dear Dr. Ray,

I encourage my children (ages ten, twelve and fifteen) to express themselves, but sometimes they get pretty hostile. I want open communication, but I don't want back talk. Is there one without the other?

Listening Too Much?

If there isn't, tact and diplomacy are headed the way of chivalry.

Encouraging some freedom of expression promotes two-way respect. A youngster feels he receives a fair hearing, and a parent feels fairer for it. Allowing unrestrained freedom of expression promotes two-way disrespect. Burne may heat up the exchange, but soon we're matching hot word for hot word. Even if we fully intend to, we can't withstand open assault for long. Our instinct for self-respect will overcome our desire for free communication. Communication without rules doesn't foster feelings; it hurts them.

Put another way, open communication does not mean license to speak one's mind in whatever tone at whatever volume with whatever words. Full freedom of opinion is benevolent parenthood; full freedom of expression is not.

As your children move deeper into adolescence and become more deeply opinionated, particularly about your conduct, you might want to establish some freedom of speech guidelines in order to promote the common good and to semi-insure domestic tranquility.

Guideline 1: Anyone can say his or her piece as long as it's said peacefully.

Guideline 2:   The speaker has the right to remain uninterrupted as long as he or she remains respectful.

Guideline 3:   As soon as communication turns ugly, the right to be heard is temporarily forfeited.

A major clarification is in order here. What constitutes disrespect is a parent's judgment. Kids have a far more tolerant definition of disrespect than we do. They don't consider themselves nasty until they're tipping tables and tossing bricks—and then only if they hit something.

Just because a rule is fair and ultimately makes for more freedom doesn't mean kids will like it.

Probably the simplest way to deal with unfeeling expression is to call a halt to it. In Congress this is called invoking cloture. (I think it comes from the Old English phrase, "Cloture mouth.") For a list of expression-halting consequences, refer to the question in chapter four on reducing back talk (page 74).

After your patient explaining of the guidelines, after your admirable refusal to respond in kind—or unkind—to disrespect, don't be too surprised if your children still think you're stifling their First Amendment rights. Just because a rule is fair and ultimately makes for more freedom doesn't mean kids will like it. It takes time to understand the benefit of such unnatural things as restraint and tact.

There is a bright side to all of this. At least the kids can take advantage of your new set of guidelines to tell you what they think of your new set of guidelines—if they do it respectfully, of course.

Word Storms

Dear Dr. Ray,

I'm a lecturer, and the kids are increasingly tuning me out. Is there hope to be heard?

Out of Tune

In the book *Back to the Family,* my associates and I interviewed parents of strong families to find out what they were doing right. We also talked to the kids to hear what they liked and didn't like about their family life. From the teens especially, the number-one disliked parenting practice was lectures. Routinely the kids admitted to drifting into a semiconscious state after about two minutes of a steady word stream. Two minutes is longer than it sounds when there's no break in the verbiage.

The propensity to lecture is a strong one and begins early in parenthood. Once, when my oldest son was about four, my wife sent him to his bed for lying. After I heard from her what had happened, I figured I'd go up and add my fatherly two cents' worth, although I think the average lecture is about sixty-eight cents' worth.

"Andrew, Mom says you lied."

"I don't remember."

"Andrew, if Mom says you lied, you lied. Now, I'm only going to ask you once for the truth. If you tell me the truth, you'll only stay here as long as Mom said. If you lie to me too, you'll stay here even longer. Now, did you lie?"

The silence was broken only by the sound of mental wheels spinning.

"I still don't remember, but if Mom says I did, there's probably a pretty good chance I did."

Ah-ha, the parenting moment I'd been anticipating: my first chance to lecture, though I'm sure that's not what I would have called it. Mentally I'd been preparing for this rite of parental passage.

"Andrew, I want to talk with you a minute." Then I gave him my best stuff. I talked about trust, about God's rules about lying, about love. I even shared a touching story from my own childhood. Yes, our souls had met. Andrew would carry this memory of his dad for life.

About eight minutes into my monologue and his silence, I stopped. "Well, Andrew, what do you think?"

"Dad?"

"Yes, Son."

"How come if I look up at the ceiling with one eye, my other eye can't look at the floor?"

Somewhere in my soul talk, I lost that boy, and I think it was probably when I said, "Andrew, I want to talk with you a minute."

Why do we persist in the face of overwhelming evidence that we're being tuned out, especially with teenagers, who are masters at turning to stone? Part of it has to do with our heart-deep drive to be good parents. We desperately want to make ourselves understood. We know why we do or don't want Rock to do something. If we can just get through to him, he'll see, learn, change and be grateful to us, sometimes even saying, "Golly, Dad, thank you for talking at me for thirty-seven straight minutes. I needed that."

Why are lectures generally so futile?

One, kids don't see parenthood through our eyes. The process of growing up takes years, and densely packed parenting words, however persuasive to us, don't do much to convince kids to think as adults. Someday most kids will, but not during a verbal storm unless it's theirs.

> **If we can just get through to him, he'll see, learn, change and be grateful to us, sometimes even saying, "Golly, Dad, thank you for talking at me for thirty-seven straight minutes. I needed that."**

Two, nobody—child or adult—likes to be on the receiving end of a droning. Further, while most lectures may begin as drones, they don't stay that way. The longer they go, the more likely they are to become tirades.

Lastly, lectures are generally spawned by an emotional situation. Somebody—usually a juvenile—has behaved poorly, and somebody else—usually the juvenile's parent—is real upset, hurt or disappointed about it. The closer in time the lecture is to the trouble, the more likely emotions are to cloud clear thinking.

OK, so we both agree that, for the most part, lectures don't work. Once in a while they may be heard and heeded, but the more words, more often the less impact. What can we do instead?

First, if you must lecture, keep it short. If it's short it probably couldn't be called a lecture. Two to three minutes should be enough to get your point across.

Second, once you've expressed your thoughts and feelings, finish by explaining what you plan to do about this particular conduct. Focusing on consequences keeps a lecture from getting personal.

Lastly, if your emotions are churning, delay the talk. Send Echo to her room while you cool. With lower emotional temperatures comes less push for steamy words.

Thank you for listening. I was hoping you would, though sometimes I'm pretty disappointed in how you react. After all I write for you, you'd think you'd care enough to read it. You know, not everybody is going to write for you all your life. You'd better get used to that fact, because I'm going to tell you something else....

Teen Tension

Dear Dr. Ray,

Please give me some ideas for getting out of arguments with my teenagers. I never win anyway.

Outwitted

By definition an argument involves two or more parties with conflicting views. So to end arguments with teens, you can (1) change your view to agree with theirs. For example, you can concur with Newton's assertion that kids who never do any homework are more likely to become Nobel Prize winners. Or (2) hold onto your opinion but don't argue with theirs. In other words, stop talking the instant you sense an argument shaping up. On average, arguments erupt about three seconds after you hear the words, "Mom, can I ask you something?"

Agreeing with teens doesn't necessarily mean you have to turn your back on reality. Much of the time agreement is your best option.

Oxford: If I have to wait until my grades come up to get a driver's license, I might as well just buy a bike now.

You: Maybe so.

Elvis: If I turn my music down any more, I might as well turn it off.

You: That'd be nice.

You're not agreeing in a sarcastic or patronizing tone. You're simply acknowledging your teen's opinion, but—and this is crucial—you're not backing away from your decision. Oxford may indeed have to put thirty-two thousand miles on his bike before he decides to change academic gears.

Out of frustration or anger at their parents' stance, kids regularly roar out their highly individual perceptions of the world. To try to convince them of the reasonableness of your view, especially while they're mad, is to get pulled into a verbal black hole. For every point you make, they'll counter with two, couched in teenage reasoning: "Music nowadays is meant to be played loud. Your music was written for the old days when times were quieter." Now I ask, how can you dispute such logic?

Another way to end word-wrangling is the closed-mouth move. You can give Wendell a gaze that silently says, "I'm not squabbling any further."

When we continue to debate with a teen, we're clinging to a small thread of a chance to win the argument. But when was the last time you won an argument with Wendell?

By "win" I mean that you got him to acknowledge even begrudgingly that your opinion had at least one molecule of merit, if only among other old folks. Kids flat out don't see life as parents do. Someday they will, but certainly not while we're arguing with them. Only in the past ten years or so have my parents and I begun to look at the world through common eyes. And I'll admit that's a bit scary for me, because they aren't getting any cooler.

There are other ways to stop talking and thereby stop arguing. You can walk away calmly. Some kids will let you leave the scene and not follow you out to the car, yelling, "And another thing," as you lock the door and crank up the radio.

If you want to reach for professional parenthood, you can master the "dumb look," an expression that nonverbally conveys, "Not only am I not going to argue, but I don't even understand what we're arguing about." This look can be used, for instance, when you hear something like, "Why should I study? The more I know, the more I forget. And the more I forget, the less I know. So why study?" Adolescents think that any adult who isn't in synch with their logic is a "space cadet" or a "buzz" or a "ditz" anyway, so we might as well play the role to our advantage.

Only in the past ten years or so have my parents and I begun to look at the world through common eyes. And I'll admit that's a bit scary for me, because they aren't getting any cooler.

One mom told me that the dumb look seemed like a smart idea to her. The only problem was that she felt dumb anytime her kids were around, and she wasn't sure they'd know when she was deliberately looking dumb or just being herself. I didn't know what to say to that, so I just gave her a dumb look.

Too Much Reasoning Is Illogical

Dear Dr. Ray,

The more I give my children the reasons behind my decisions, the more they ask "why" about everything. Should I continue giving them my reasons?

Out of Answers

Why? Just give me one good reason why you should.

Kids are true child psychologists, always six steps ahead of us grown-ups. When we ask Kitty why she threw the cat onto the roof, invariably we hear, "I don't know." But when she repeatedly badgers us why she can't play with Sylvester anymore today, we feel obliged to offer fifteen different answers in the vain hope of hitting on one she'll approve of.

Giving kids the reasons underlying our discipline is wise practice. It tells them that there is method to our madness and that we're not simply bucking for a "Tyrant-Parent-of-the-Decade" award. We actually do have a rationale for wanting the trash hauled out before the bacteria multiply enough to eat a hole in the bag.

Giving kids the reasons for our discipline becomes unwise—not to mention nerve-racking—when we start repeating ourselves. What parent hasn't in total exasperation finally bellowed, "Because I'm your mother, that's why," or, "Because I said so," or the wonderfully elegant, "Because." The first time we fired these off we shuddered to hear ourselves sounding just like our parents. Back then we promised aloud, "I'll never say that to my kids." What we didn't realize then and what our own youngsters don't realize now is that kids can receive fifteen logical answers as to why curfew is midnight, each of which they will dispute until Mom or Dad, hitting the limits of human endurance, explodes with, "Because I said so."

If he agreed with all your parenting moves, he wouldn't need you. He could raise himself.

No doubt you've reviewed for Ripley the reasons for all your rules and requirements hundreds, maybe thousands of times; that was when he was still a preschooler. It's not that he doesn't believe or understand your motives. He just doesn't agree with them or like them or appreciate them. Can you really expect him to? He's a kid. If he agreed with all your parenting moves, he wouldn't need you to teach him values. He'd see child rearing from a parent's perspective. He could raise himself.

If Sherlock asks you more than once why he can't stay overnight at Watson's house, that's a dead giveaway that he's not really interested in your reasons. He wants to debate. His motto is "Keep Mom answering until she wears down." He knows what he's doing. Have you *ever* answered fourteen "why's" or "why not's" in a row, and on number fourteen seen Sherlock's face light up? "Gosh, Mom. I've been so stubborn. Thank you for explaining it to me. I admire your patience."

So is it wise to provide reasons for everything you do? Yes—once, or maybe twice if you suspect you weren't heard the first time around. More than that is just begging for an argument. To short-circuit any further inquisitions, you might reply with, "I gave you my reason. You didn't like it," and then say no more. Or you could use a line popularized in the workplace: "What part of 'No' don't you understand?"

Obviously, on complex issues such as smoking or driving privileges, discussions are in order. But on most day-to-day matters, I'm sure you've explained yourself ragged. Why drag through the same verbal ritual each and every time it's Madge's turn to clear the table, or Taylor has to put his jacket in the closet instead of over the sink? Here no explanations at all are called for; discipline is. ◦

If at First You Don't Succeed

Dear Dr. Ray,
Sometimes I think I'm handling a situation really well, and then it all blows up in my face.

Shell-Shocked

Some years ago I was playing in a softball tournament. A five-year-old boy walked up behind me and with his bat took a few swings at my legs. Since I'm allergic to aluminum smacking my body at forty miles an hour—I break out in red welts—I said to the young Babe, "That's enough of that. Can it." I'm professionally trained to communicate with children.

My teammates immediately took their swings. "Hey, Mr. Psycho-man knows kids. 'Can it.' He's too smooth."

Forced to prove that I am no rinky-dink shrink, I rushed to my car and grabbed my Psychology 605 textbook, a thick tome on how to handle any kid, anywhere, anytime. (The book is always in my trunk. One never knows when an emergency roadside healing will be required.) After memorizing the section on bat-wielding five-year-olds, I returned ready to take control.

First I bent down close to the little guy. As the veterinarians recommend, "Don't tower over a wild animal. Let him smell you." Next came my expression of feelings: "I don't like being hit with a ball bat." Translation: I'm not comfortable with where your bat is coming from. I can't go with that.

Then I set up some natural consequences: "If you swing at me, I'll just walk away." In essence: you swing, no target, no game, no fun. As I spoke I slowly guided his bat to the ground. After all, it's important to keep your verbal and nonverbal cues in synch. Otherwise you'll send mixed messages.

Finally, my deal closer. "Please put the bat down, and we'll play catch with my softball." I put the little scamp on an informal contingency contract, with a variable ratio reinforcement schedule and maximum response effectiveness. In one thirty-seven-second mini-speech, I covered about five therapeutic techniques. This poor child was set to be putty in my hands.

All I can assume is that he didn't read my Psych 605 textbook. No sooner had I shared my final communication strategy than he shared his: "Yeah, right. Get real, Jerk Face."

Maybe I should have stuck with "Can it," though I did learn something critical: It isn't good psychology to grade a technique after one try. If a child is involved in the scenario, two other variables are added: unpredictability and time—lots of time.

When you're convinced you're handling trouble well—staying calm, reasonable, resolute—most likely you are. That doesn't guarantee all will resolve immediately or peacefully. Kids are not consistently rational creatures (who is?), particularly when being disciplined. So your maturity doesn't guarantee their maturity.

The first few dozen, maybe hundred times you react with calm firmness to a situation, you may not be rewarded. It is the cumulative effect of good parenting over time that brings good results, for you and the kids.

I guess that's why, after my professionally choreographed series of interchanges, I did not hear, "Why, thank you, Sir. I most certainly am sorry for swinging at you. Please accept my apology, and I would love to interact with you and the softball in a mutually satisfactory way."

Actually, I think I would have been more shocked had I heard this than "Yeah, right…"

Perfectly Reasonable

Dear Dr. Ray,

*My daughter, age sixteen, accuses, "You expect me to be perfect,"
if I discipline her or put limits on her freedom. I want to be reasonable
in my expectations.*

Imperfect Parent

Well, *do* you expect her to be perfect? I would hope so. Any expectation for responsible and moral conduct is attached to some ideal to strive toward. Disciplining your daughter for disrespect implies that you expect respect—all the time, not just some of the time. Grounding her for abusing curfew indicates you have curfew rules in place for every night, not just for Tuesdays and the second Thursday following a full moon.

Most likely your daughter is not actually accusing you of demanding perfection; she is just complaining about those rules she doesn't like. She may be calling your expectations "perfect" when she really means "too high in my opinion." For instance, if you punish her for mistreating a sibling, she views this as not allowing her to make a mistake or to act badly—in other words, to be human. If you were being reasonable, you'd understand that even the best of people do wrong things, and you'd give her some slack.

To expect perfect behavior is not to expect someone to be perfect. It is to establish a standard to teach by.

Indeed, you are being reasonable, perfectly so. To expect perfect behavior is not to expect someone to be perfect. It is to establish a standard to teach by.

I want my kids' rooms orderly. Are they? What do you think? Even as I enforce my room rules, I am aware that the rooms will never be kept to my liking, much less perfectly so. This does not mean that I don't hold to some kind of ideal. Further, my standard may, in fact, not be all that high, but compared to my kids' standard, it's in the stratosphere.

This brings me to a second point. If your daughter's idea of what constitutes good teenage conduct is lower than yours—and I'll bet it is—then she's accusing you of being a perfectionist not because you are but because you expect more of her than she does. Which means, in her opinion, your standards are not just higher than hers but higher than most anybody's. Teens have a proclivity for seeing their way as the only reasonable way.

Then too, when was the last time your daughter thought you eminently fair for disciplining her? Yesterday? Last year? When she was three? It is a truth of life that kids—and even most adults—often can justify their behavior in their own minds enough to excuse it from any consequences. If another person, especially one in authority, doesn't quite agree with their thinking, he or she is being intolerant of fallible human nature.

Can you use my arguments on your daughter? Are you kidding? What are you, a perfectionist? You can use them on yourself, though, to feel less guilty and vulnerable to your daughter's accusations.

When will your daughter come to appreciate your so-called perfectionism? When she's paying her own bills? When she has teenagers? When she's perfect?

There is an irony in all this. Because of your discipline, your daughter sees you as demanding perfection. What she doesn't see is that this very discipline is making her a better person. And the better she gets, the more she'll come to see how far we all are from perfection.

So Did You

Dear Dr. Ray,

How do you respond to an adolescent boy who, upon being disciplined, says, "You did the same things when you were my age"?

Dumber Then

Before we respond to your son, permit me to respond to you. How did he know you did the same things when you were his age? Who told him? Whoever it was inadvertently has made your parenting tougher. There is a point where communication from parent—or grandparent—to child can be too open.

But since he now knows, don't provide any more details. Your past, however wrong or stupid, is not his concern unless you wish it to be. But remember, whatever you say can and may be held against you.

Now let us respond to your son. Know above all that your moral authority as a parent does not depend one whit upon your moral conduct as a child. If it did, few of us could claim full parental status. The very process of maturing dictates that we are more foolish and short-sighted when younger. However you wish to convey to your son this absolute truth, do so. But don't expect him to understand or agree. That's part of his immaturity. Nevertheless, by making this point—as briefly as possible, by the way—you are in essence saying,

> **Your moral authority as a parent does not depend one whit upon your moral conduct as a child.**

"My resolve will not be weakened, nor any guilt caused, by childhood illogic."

Next, admit that you were indeed a child. "You're right, I did teenager things when I was a teenager." Keep any admissions deliberately vague. Even though you refuse to be manipulated, no sense giving your son more fodder about your past to keep chewing on.

Point three: Contrary to what your son thinks, you are not so old as to recall only in a misty haze what impulses, desires and dangers accompany youth. It is your memory of having lived once at his age that makes you acutely aware of your duty to help him safely navigate those same waters. Part of being a good parent is knowing the reality of being bad as a kid.

Now, on to your masterstroke. With no shame, tell your son that he is very lucky that you too once did wrong and bad things—though not anymore, of course. It is that very misconduct that is driving you to be the strong and vigilant parent you are today. Through your firsthand, personal experience with wrong behavior, you realize how critical it is that you protect him from potential foolishness and discipline him for actual foolishness. Whatever you might have once gotten away with was not to your benefit.

If you really want to be irksome, you can say, "You are right. I did do the same things when I was your age. But my duty right now is to raise the best kid I can. And that means raising a person who is better than I was."

There's not much that bugs a teen more than a parent who compliments at the same time she disciplines.

THREE

More Authority = Less Discipline

Parenthood is packed with irony. During the teen years most of us need to be at our child-rearing strongest. The typical teen is more savvy and willful than even the toughest preschooler. And the discipline issues are a lot more complex than figuring out who kicked over the toy blocks.

But this is often when many of us are losing discipline steam. We've been at this now for at least twelve years. Just when we're hoping to gear down our guidance, discipline and supervision, this parenting journey is forcing us to ramp up all three.

Well, if we don't have quite the energy and stamina we had when we were younger, we'd better find some ways to compensate. A prime way is to increase our authority, because stronger authority—calm, confident, composed—means less discipline effort and ultimately better kids.

Better Late Than Never

Dear Dr. Ray,

My son is fifteen. I've been a weak disciplinarian since he was little. Is it too late for me to change, for his sake and mine?

Slow Learner Mom

It's too late to change ourselves when this life is over. Short of that, improvement is always possible. That said, sometimes the odds of our change making much difference may be low. Nevertheless, you must act in the hopes of success, no matter what the reality might be.

Let's say your doctor has just discovered that you have been eating foods that are damaging your stomach. How do you react to this revelation? You stop eating those foods immediately, even if you're not sure your stomach will respond. At the least you want no further damage; at best you want to heal.

At some point in their child rearing, most parents become aware if they've been moving in a bad direction. The evidence accumulates over time. Unfortunately for many, awareness doesn't necessarily lead to change. But for those for whom it does, there is bad news and good news. The bad news: the longer-lived the problems, the slower and harder the improvement. The good news: The chances of success are much higher now than they were before the change of direction.

In your situation the bad news: Your son is not eight years old. The good news: He's not eighteen.

So once you start to change, how will he change? First in behavior; later in attitude.

Suppose you establish a new house rule: All chores and duties (including schoolwork) must be satisfactorily completed before any privileges begin. Your son—once he comes **Actions can be** to believe this new you is really you and not **changed much** some alien life force controlling his **more quickly** mother's body—most likely will start to **than minds.** comply within weeks, even days, but only because he is feeling forced to and only because it is in his own self-interest.

For a while your son will be more convinced than ever that you are unreasonable, dictatorial or arbitrary—and these are your good qualities. Such is to be expected. Actions can be changed much more quickly than minds. Many of your son's wrongheaded views are years old. You aren't going to right them in two months.

When will his attitude start to improve? I don't know (I get paid for this). But I do know that if you persevere through his resistance,

Stepford Child compliance may eventually become respectful cooperation. That is your ultimate goal.

There are other critical reasons to reverse your parenting, even if it seems late. And their number corresponds exactly to the number of younger brothers and sisters. They see what trails you are blazing with Big Brother. You didn't mention other siblings, but if they are there, they are watching you closely. Change those trails now, and you will change theirs too. And then "Is it too late?" won't need to be asked again.

Reversing Directions

Dear Dr. Ray,

Having realized that I've been a lax disciplinarian for years, should I change all at once or gradually?

Coming to My Senses

Change all at once. That's the best way. Alas, in so doing, you will change only gradually. Even trying with all your might, it's nearly impossible to change quickly and fully. Your parenting style and habits have the momentum of several years. Suddenly slamming on the brakes and reversing engines won't result in an immediate 180-degree turnabout. Most likely you'll skid for a while, inch to a halt and then slowly reverse directions.

Altering a ship's course is child's play compared to altering a parenting course.

Turning around a large ship in the ocean takes up to twelve miles. And that's a ship without kids. You're not the size of a ship, but you're far more complex. Altering a ship's course is child's play compared to altering a parenting course.

Nevertheless, you need to begin changing your ways right now and with full speed ahead. First, the longer you delay, the longer bad habits have to further harden. Breaking bad habits a little at a time is like trying to quit smoking a little at a time. You're struggling to conquer the same behavior in which you keep indulging.

Second, changing gradually leads to changing erratically. Let's say you prioritize your list of trouble. This month you'll tackle the majors: back talk, defiance and sibling quibbling. Next month you'll move on to clothes debris, phone time and chores. What if you're still getting resistance in the big three at the end of the month? Do you allot another month, thus still ignoring the "minor" issues? And when is a problem conquered? At 50 percent less? 75 percent? In fact, most misbehavior never completely goes away. So if you wait until one problem is all gone, you'll never move on to any others.

Third, the faces of misconduct overlap. For example, back talk and defiance may be intertwined with phone trouble. Sibling quibbling can lead to chore hassles and vice versa. You can't deal effectively with one without simultaneously dealing with the others.

Fourth, bad stuff needs to be stopped now. When you sense you're drinking spoiled milk, do you slow your rate of swallowing or spit it out? If your child were doing something harmful, would you allow him three months to give it up? One of the greater human blessings is self-awareness. Once we realize we're heading in the wrong direction, we can exert all our will to change course if we so choose.

So how will your kids react to the new you? They'll be shell-shocked. Who is this stranger? What kind of junk has she been reading? How long is this going to last until we get back to normal?

Kids don't generally realize what is good for them, so they resist it. That's all right. Shortly they'll come to accept the fact that this stronger parent is here to stay and will only get stronger with time. And gradually they'll change, too, into more mature human beings who'll learn to appreciate the way things have changed.

Pendulum Parenting

Dear Dr. Ray,

As a teenager I experienced harsh and erratic discipline. I'm so afraid of doing the same to my kids (ages fourteen and fifteen) that I tend toward being permissive and lax.

Overcompensator

The opposite of harsh is not permissive; it is lovingly strong. The opposite of erratic is not lax; it is consistent.

The drive to parent opposite from any hurtful ways you were raised is a common and powerful one. In part this is because emotional reactions of years ago may linger today. They can evoke potent memories of feeling misunderstood and mistreated. Consequently, to make sure that you don't provoke the same feelings in your kids, you scrupulously seek to avoid disagreements or conflict. The primary goal of your parenting is peace, even when your better judgment says to stand your ground in the face of resistance.

There are two unavoidable traps lurking in this parenting style. One, it is not possible to avoid upsetting kids. The very reality of socializing a child means you must make many decisions—good ones—that they will find disagreeable, unfair, arbitrary or "mean." And yes, at times they may even believe *you* are disagreeable, unfair, arbitrary or "mean." You must be ready to "cause" in your children some *temporary*—that is the key word—feelings of being misunderstood or mistreated. Otherwise you pretty much must let them decide for themselves how to run their own lives, even at ages fourteen and fifteen.

Herein lies trap number two. Even if you can sidestep conflict for the moment, over time you will only cause more conflict. Quite simply, you never can parent in a way your kids will always find fair and agreeable. In due course, more and more of your decisions, no matter how compromising, will anger them.

Why? Because Core Law of Human Nature Number 103 says that you can't satisfy consistently other people—big or little—by giving in to their every desire. They will become only harder to please, trickier to get along with and more demanding. They will become more easily reactive to the slightest whiff that you are not doing things their way.

The opposite of harsh parenting is strong parenting. It is calm, loving resolve.

The final irony? The very thing you so desperately want to avoid—a harsh and erratic relationship with your children—you risk creating. They don't appreciate your parenting looseness, as they've come to want more and more looseness in order to be pacified. At the same time you fight feelings of frustration and impotence, as no matter how much you try to see things their way, you never get credit for it.

So how do you avoid this spiraling cycle?

First, drive this notion into your head: The opposite of harsh parenting is strong parenting. It is calm, loving resolve. To be firm in your decisions is not in the least mean or dictatorial. It is doing well by your children—now and in the future.

Second, your kids' unreasonable reaction to your limits and rules is not an automatic indicator that you are being unreasonable. There is a huge difference between unfair discipline and discipline that kids might think is unfair. In loving homes a teen's bad reactions to rules are not usually a reliable indicator that the rules are bad.

Finally, consider this. In all likelihood your parents didn't give much thought to their approach and its effect on you. They did what they did, for better or worse. The fact that you are so concerned about your behavior reflects a desire to be a good parent. In and of itself, this is pretty good evidence that your style is not harsh or erratic. Indeed, one way to be harsh is to be so afraid of doing so that you don't allow yourself to be strong and consistent.

It's Only a Stage

Dear Dr. Ray,

I've recently realized that I need to take a firmer discipline stand with my kids, but they don't seem to be taking me seriously. It's as though they're just waiting for me to go back to my old self.

A New Woman, Really

They are. Kids are natural-born skeptics, at least where discipline is concerned. They will settle for nothing less than time and consistency from us before being convinced that our new resolve is for real.

Wise parents make adjustments, sometimes big ones. Routinely a mother or father will call me, spurred on by the realization that "something has to change" in the home. The kids have become the heads of the household, and the parents are hostages to increasing misbehavior. (Is "misbehavior" a politically incorrect child-rearing term? I think I hear an expert somewhere intoning, "There is no misbehavior, only misunderstood behavior.")

Generally, the younger a child when a parent decides that limits are also love, the shorter and less bumpy the road back to a parent-centered household. All too sadly, many parents need ten to fifteen years of increasingly being abused to conclude that they've let their authority slip away. Then life becomes the child's dominant parent, teaching lessons far more roughly than moms and dads do, even in our firmest discipline moments.

The kids have become the heads of the household, and the parents are hostages to increasing misbehavior.

I wholeheartedly applaud your insight, and you didn't even have to pay some therapist big bucks for it. Now you have two hurdles ahead of you. One, to maintain, hopefully build upon, your newfound determination. And two, to convince your kids this reborn mother is just the beginning. Fortunately, if you do the first, the second will take care of itself.

As you've seen, initially kids aren't inclined to take the new you seriously. "What is this? Did you see some shrink on *Oprah* today, Mom?" "Did you go buy some new parenting book?" Parents often tell me, after seeing me a few times, that their kids are asking, "Who have you been talking to?"

Come to think of it, the kids are insulting us. The implication is that we aren't capable of changing ourselves on our own. There must be some hidden influence somewhere prodding us to be more self-assured, and once that's gone, our spines will return to Styrofoam.

You could play with your kids' heads a bit. Tape a copy of this page to the refrigerator. They'll think it's the source of your strength. Most likely it will mysteriously disappear. Tape up another, knowing it too will be swiped in a few days. Whereupon your kids will settle back, confident that your phase is about to pass now that the shrink has been eliminated, only to find with time that your resolve is internal and not taped to a door. They've learned a lesson about doubting their mother.

In a way, who can blame kids for being skeptical about discipline changes? Almost on a weekly basis, parents "have had it up to here" and resolve that "there are going to be some changes around here, young man." Then Bruno knows to lower his unruly profile a while until we get back to status quo. The effect of this cycle is that we lose a little credibility each time we enter it and don't live it through. So when you've finally, really, truly, actually had enough, you'd better be prepared to prove it for a long time—in fact, for the rest of their childhood.

The relationship is simple: If you keep your resolve, the kids will believe. If you think it'll help, you could tell them, "You know, you guys are right. This is a phase I'm going through. It will be about fifteen years long."

The Authority Test

Dear Dr. Ray,

I used to think I was a pretty strong parent, but I'm beginning to wonder. As my children have gotten older, they're resisting my discipline with more intensity.

Shaky Mom

Want a simple test of parental authority? Next time your child does something wrong or bad—wait, I must briefly digress.

Can we still use words like *bad* or *wrong* in our value-neutral culture? Must we morally antisepticize the language, as some experts assert? "Blade, putting the ice pick in your sister's foot is inappropriate conduct." No, it's real bad conduct. Just ask his sister.

So when your youngster next acts badly or wrongly, set up a field experiment. In an even tone of voice, one time, levy a consequence: "Eve, you are being very disrespectful. Head for your room; your night is over." "I asked you three times to clean the bathroom, Hazel. You ignored me all three times. You now have two hours of labor. Let's begin immediately." "Webster, you will write a four-hundred-word apology to your teacher for getting a detention in her class." "Because you called your little brother a name, Oral, you will give him two dollars."

Once only, calmly, discipline. Then step back and observe what happens. Is there cooperation? a look of disbelief? relentless negotiation and defense? an outright argument? a look saying, "I'll comply, but you and everybody else will pay for the next six hours"? a fit? stomping? more misbehavior? leaving the time-out corner twenty-six times? a posture that says, "You and what army?"

Put simply, how does your child react? In large measure this will tell you how he views your authority. I am convinced that a child's response when disciplined is more affected by his perception of his parent than by his temperament.

Routinely parents call children strong-willed who are not. Their conduct is emboldened by their perception of Mom or Dad as weak-willed. In essence, the more a youngster believes that our discipline is questionable or challengeable, the stronger will be his resistance to it.

A child's response when disciplined is more affected by his perception of his parent than by his temperament.

So how do parents overall score on the authority test? As a discipline teacher for over twenty-five years, my results say that the average American parent with the average American child does not get cooperation without resistance, ranging from verbal to physical. If by nature Butkus has always been easy or mature or compliant, then he usually cooperates with discipline on his own. But if he is normal-natured or stronger, getting resistance is more common than acceptance for most moms and dads.

So how did *you* do? What did your kids do? There is good news and bad news. The bad news: if the kids resisted, in word or deed, you can conclude pretty safely that they don't see you as having confident, legitimate authority. The good news: You can change this perception if you change you.

I believe without a doubt that a generation or two ago, more parents passed the test. Why? Again, perception. Kids viewed parents—indeed, most grown-ups—as having legitimate authority. That's because the grown-ups also viewed themselves that way and acted accordingly. The irony is that if a parent has authority in a child's mind, she doesn't have to assert it very often; it's a given. If she doesn't have authority in the child's mind, she is always trying to assert some weak form of it, usually with words or emotion.

So what can parents do to change a child's perception and slowly reestablish themselves as the resolute, loving leaders of their home? Allow this story about my wife to illustrate.

A few years back my son Andrew asked his mother, "Mom, what would you do if you told me to do something and I just refused?" At age fifteen, a weightlifter and feeling a bit like a young stallion, he knew he was now physically the second-strongest person in the house. (His twelve-year-old sister was first.)

My wife responded, "Andrew, I'd have to shut you down. All of your privileges, activities, favorite foods and electrical goods would cease until you cooperate willingly."

Andrew's move: "But what if you grounded me like that and I just walked out?"

Randi's move, checkmate: "Oh, that's different. Then I would do two things. First, I'd cry because I love you so much. Then I would blow my nose and call the police."

"Mom, you know I wouldn't do anything like that." But if he did, she would call because she does love him so much and because she will *not* permit a child to defy her authority.

Many times I've suggested to parents a technique called "blackout." Let's say you assign your daughter a five-hundred-word essay on respect in response to her nasty or disdainful tone. She responds with some version of, "Yeah, right. Like I'm going to do that." You now have two options.

One, find another consequence she'll agree with and accept. Good luck.

Two, show her that you are willing to stand even stronger. Implement blackout. Blackout is immediate cessation of all perks and privileges—except love, food and, OK, the bathroom—until you get the consequence you initially levied.

How will Bliss get to soccer practice? All her transportation is shut down until you get the essay—which is now longer, as she refused to accept your initial length. She has no phone privileges to call anyone for a ride and no computer to e-mail friends of her plight. She can't even cry to neighbors for help, as she's not allowed outside. There are simply no activities except school, reading and chores.

Gone too are the television, radio, CD player. If she uses any of her own possessions of entertainment, they are taken—for a time or forever, your call. As for school, Bliss now has to pack her own lunch, as there is no money supply; it too is shut off. Even eating out is a privilege, so though Bliss must go with you when the family goes out, she eats at home before you all leave.

All kids misbehave—lots. But when a child blatantly challenges your parenting by refusing to accept legitimate discipline, he has intensified his misbehavior dramatically. This is where a parent has to be at her most confident and resolute. Blackout is one way to convey the fact that you see defiance as a serious offense.

Red Corvette Discipline

Dear Dr. Ray,

What do you think about a parent's saying, "I can't wait until he can drive. Then I'll have something to hang over his head to make him behave"?

Automatic

I think, "Well, buy him a red Corvette when he turns sixteen, and then you'll really have something to hang over his head."

Alas, not even a red Corvette can make a parent a good disciplinarian. Nevertheless, out of frustration and feelings of helplessness with their teen, some parents hope for future leverage toward a little cooperation. But such hope is not founded upon reality.

First, if a parent believes that future privileges will foster discipline that "works," what does that say about his authority now? Has he lost it, and if so, how much has he lost? The more authority a parent has let slip away, the less likely removing upcoming privileges, however valued by a child, will bring about much positive change. In fact, such discipline is likely to be a new source of conflict, as Mario may get really mad if Mom messes with something as precious as the car keys.

If in his eyes she had no past right to take away his stuff, why would she have any present right, especially now that he's older?

Second, even if A.J. does become more pleasant, what is his motive? Is it solely to get and keep driving status? If holding on to one big privilege is the driving force behind treating his parents better, what happens if and when he loses that privilege? What big stick is left to Mom or Dad? Healthy authority is never founded upon one or two consequences, no matter how powerful they might be.

Healthy authority is never founded upon one or two consequences, no matter how powerful they might be.

Third, discipline teaches better when it removes more than just excess. Nowadays many teens' existence is a mini Disney World. So if Mickey gets mouthy and loses his PlayStation, no big deal. That still leaves untouched the computer, TV, stereo, four-wheeler, semiannual cruise and beach home in Florida. When a child is "disciplined" by having 8 percent of a 97 percent excess cut out, he will learn slowly. True, driving might be a big-ticket item; nonetheless, it is still part of a long-standing pattern of taking away only part of way too much anyway.

Fourth, driving is a privilege to be earned, not an entitlement of age, as most kids, even many parents, seem to believe. The foremost question to ask is, "Has Ford shown himself mature enough to deserve wheels under him?" If a parent is counting on car access as the ultimate discipline leverage, the question has been answered: Here is a youngster who is not ready to drive. There is no reason even to consider "having something to hang over his head" because he doesn't deserve having the something in the first place.

A closing thought: When a child is responsible with current privileges, then the parent can contemplate new ones. It is seldom wise to give new goodies and perks when the old ones haven't yet taught the lessons.

No More Room

Dear Dr. Ray,

I've heard, "Don't send children to their rooms for punishment. It only pairs something negative with someplace that should be positive."

Where to Now?

Wow. I must be messed up and don't realize it. I was sent to my room countless times growing up. Whatever "bad room feelings" I might have developed were either repressed—at least until I uncover them on some upcoming visit to a midday TV talk show—or else overcome by all the good feelings created by sleep, privacy, reading and naps.

I have never met any adult traumatized or even residually distressed over spending involuntary room time as a kid.

Indeed, I have never met any adult traumatized or even residually distressed over spending involuntary room time as a kid. You'd think with all the folks I encounter in clinical practice, I'd bump into a few with leftover room angst as at least a small part of their adult troubles.

What you've heard I will label Child-rearing Cliché Number Twenty-seven. It is part of a larger "enlightened" assault on traditional forms of discipline: spanking breeds aggression; corners are humiliating; time-out is isolating; writing essays fosters distaste for English; fining a child money breaks trust, as it "takes back" a promised allowance.

All of these I've encountered from "experts." Is anything left that is psychologically OK to use? How about taking away privileges or possessions? Well, that depends, goes the argument. Are they gifts from another person? Did Macey pay for them herself? Are they related to the crime? How long will they be taken? Was Forbes sufficiently warned?

Most anything that can serve as a discipline consequence also has other uses. I like chairs a lot. I'm sitting on one now. Do I want to sit on one facing a corner? No, that's boring.

I'm writing at this moment, making money doing it. Do I want to be forced to write something about my misbehavior on my own time—for free? Nope.

I use rulers to measure things. They're invaluable for household repairs. Was a ruler used to measure my behind a few times as a kid? Yep. Am I afraid of rulers now? Not at all, unless they're career politicians.

Most places and things can be good or bad, helpful or hurtful, depending upon the context in which they are used. Further, except in the most extreme cases, contexts don't overlap. One doesn't color the other. Involuntary room time doesn't spoil voluntary room time.

Much of what makes discipline effective is the factor of choice. If Nielson just so happens to be too busy to watch TV for two days, he doesn't feel deprived. It was his decision. If you punish him by suspending TV for two days, he does feel the effect.

If Knap retreats to his bed for a two-hour snooze, he's content. If you send him there two hours early for bed, he's discontent. Time, place and freedom of will make all the difference in seeing something as reward or as punishment.

To further drive the point home, try this exercise. Next time Butkus acts up, give him a choice: He can either wash the car or go to his room for an hour. See which he chooses. See if he's pleased to be given the option. And see if the room isn't the more desirable place to be. It's all in the timing.

Lengthening Your Fuse

Dear Dr. Ray,

How can I discipline my children without getting angry? I find myself becoming easily frustrated with my sons, ages nine and thirteen.

Trip Switch

There's a lot of subtle pressure on parents these days to practice 100 percent anger-free child rearing. Resist the pressure; it can't be done. No parent disciplines without getting angry sometimes.

I do recall one mom who was determined to stay calm from day one of motherhood. She was hospitalized with an ulcer, but her sixteen-month-old was allowed to visit her.

Anytime your emotions are wrapped tightly around another human being, you will do emotional things, like say words not meant, lose control and yell. Emotions, even negative ones, are signs of close involvement. This said, most of us admit we could do a calmer job of child raising and, in particular, disciplining.

If a youngster misbehaves only once per day (let me study this child), in sixteen years the total of misbehaviors is over five thousand.

Consider the parenting debut. On day one we are blessed with a being with zero social skills. It is completely self-centered. It wants what it wants the second it wants it, becoming a raving emotional lunatic if it doesn't get it.

Over the better part of the next two decades, we will strive to permeate this child with self-control, maturity and morals. In the meantime we will face thousands upon thousands of episodes of resistant, obnoxious, difficult, thoughtless, moody, selfish behavior. This isn't a negative picture. It's reality. It's childhood. And lest you think that "thousands upon thousands" is an overstatement, consider that if a youngster misbehaves only once per day (let me study this child), in sixteen years the total of misbehaviors is over five thousand.

Most parents grasp this fact intellectually; we forget it emotionally. But the more we understand and accept it, the better we'll be able to confront it when it presents itself daily, even hourly or by the minute.

In no way am I implying that we should tolerate or overlook conduct that deserves discipline. We must handle it with all the love and resolve we can muster. Just knowing and expecting that misbehavior is coming, though, can reduce the frustration when it arrives.

A great definition of stress is "the difference between the way we'd like things to be and the way that they are." To the degree that we expect a Hallmark card family scene with an ever-cooperative and grateful Chastity and Oxford walking with us, we will be frustrated and wonder, "What's wrong?" When kids misbehave, most of the time there is nothing wrong. They're being kids, and they're forcing us to be parents.

Nonetheless, there are techniques to help us be calmer parents.

Technique Number One: Act early in the chain. An all-too-typical discipline scene unfolds like this: Butkus ignores, defies or debates parent. Parent repeats, prods, argues, threatens. Butkus resists further, talks tougher, escalates. Parent stands ground, gets upset, disciplines. The whole scenario takes twenty-seven minutes to intensify. By the time the parent finally disciplines, the misbehavior has multiplied, words have clashed, emotions have flared. Who wouldn't be frustrated at this point?

Don't allow the exchange to get on a roll. Discipline early, when it is warranted and while you're still calm. Believe it or not, Butkus will accept his discipline more quietly. To keep frustration lower, act more quickly.

Technique Number Two: Get out of each other's faces. As soon as you feel your temperature rise a few degrees, send Butkus to his room, or you go to yours. The situation will still be dealt with, only later when you're back to 98.6 degrees. Distance is a great sedative. It helps clear minds, stabilize reasoning and soften words.

Technique Number Three: Delay. If a particular problem or misbehavior is unexpected, baffling or worrisome, it doesn't need to be faced instantly. The deed is done, and there's no real hurry to correct it. Put a little time between your discovery of the misconduct and your response to it. Like distance, time tranquilizes emotions—not all the way but enough to balance your feelings with thoughts.

Technique Number Four: Drop your voice. John Wayne's acting advice is sound advice for parents: talk low, talk slow. Force yourself to speak more deliberately even as you feel less deliberate.

It's a maxim of behavior that sometimes the action determines the emotion. When you don't feel calm, take a deep breath and act calm. The emotion may follow suit. At the very least, your kids will wonder what's wrong with you. Maybe you snapped, and now who knows what kind of discipline you'll concoct. Quiet talk is not only more credible; it gets attention.

No parent can ever be calm all the time. Nor do I think you would want to be. Emotion makes a strong statement. The problem comes when emotion rules too often.

Fortunately, our level of frustration is not determined solely by our kids, though it may seem so. We can turn up or down our daily exasperation through our attitude and our approach. A great thing about parenthood is that we are not pawns to our kids' behavior. We don't have to get mad every time they act badly. Indeed, our behavior influences theirs more than theirs does ours. The big challenge is that usually we have to change first.

Time to Work

Dear Dr. Ray,

How about some ideas for finding discipline that works?

Impatient

It all depends upon what you mean by "works." Almost all discipline works—and immediately—in that it teaches a lesson. It says to Sherlock, "If you do A, I'll do B." Elementary.

This is not, however, how most people define "discipline that works." What they mean is a technique or strategy that changes Watson's behavior for the better, and fast. Though this is a desirable goal, in reality it often leads to undesirable results. It can cause pinball parenting: bounding from idea to idea in search of that one that will cure instantly the maddeningly repetitive misconduct.

"I've tried everything; nothing works. I have talked until I'm hoarse, taken away his favorite CD until 2056, used seventeen different reward systems, promised him an all-expenses-paid trip to Disney World, threatened grounding with backup banishment to Siberia. Finally I got totally frustrated. I sent him on an errand to the neighbor's and moved while he was gone."

As parents lament to me all they've tried, and in their minds fruitlessly, I find that they tried plenty that would have worked, given time. They mistakenly assumed that if they didn't see results in short order, they must have been on the wrong track. Not necessarily so. The discipline was working, just not as quickly as they had hoped or expected.

OK, but don't different kids respond differently to different techniques? Sure. Maybe Macy would do absolutely anything to avoid losing her favorite sweatshirt for a week, while Levi doesn't know the difference between a sweatshirt and sweat socks. On the other hand, the thought of writing a two-hundred-word essay on his misconduct makes Levi sweat bullets. Certainly some discipline "works" more or less quickly for some kids than others, but almost all discipline needs more time to change a child's behavior than grown-ups would like. Such is the nature of discipline and kids.

Discipline is a process, not a fix. So am I trying to weasel out of giving you an answer to your question? Well, whatever works. Actually, there are a few general principles to keep in mind in searching for discipline that works.

1. Keep it simple. Repetition is what makes discipline work. And it's hard to persevere with complicated consequences. Pick stuff you can use for most trouble: monetary fines, extra chores, writing sentences or essays, room time, remodeling the attic (just kidding). Then be ready to "repeat as necessary."

2. Be patient. God gives us a lifetime to work on our behavior. We can give the kids a few years to work on theirs. Discipline is a process, not a fix.

3. Hold the course. Almost any thoughtful consequence will work—that is, change the behavior—given enough parental perseverance. I know, you want to retire in thirty-one years. But believe it or not, time is your ally. Good, steady discipline does teach good behavior, even while your child is still a child.

A Lifetime of Discipline

Dear Dr. Ray,

I think I'm pretty consistent in disciplining my son (age thirteen), yet he still gets into trouble for the same things over and over. Why does it seem to take so long for discipline to work?

Still Waiting

Kids repel discipline. Being held accountable for their actions is not high on their list of favorite things in life. Conventional child-rearing wisdom says, "Children want discipline. They want the security of knowing there are rules and limits to live by." I agree, when they're grown-up and can look back with a longer perspective: "Now I'm starting to understand why my parents (teachers, grandpa, aunt) did what they did."

But at the time it's happening—at the moment of experiencing the repercussions of his behavior—discipline is not something a child wants. When was the last time you overheard your son suggesting to his friend, "Hey, Igor, why don't you come over to my mom's house and we can let her discipline us awhile?"

In their more rational, away-from-discipline moments, kids may acknowledge the need for discipline and even be slightly grateful here and there. But right as it's about to affect them, they'll do what they can to avoid or escape it. And should that surprise us? Children don't understand the long-range purpose behind most of our parenting. They look at the now and see that we're doing something they totally disagree with.

When was the last time your son ventured out of his room after half an hour there for disrespectful talk and said, "Mom, can I talk to you a minute? I was thinking, while I was stuck in my room, watching those guys play football outside without me on the last nice day of the year. Oh, yeah, I could have a mom like Lucky's mom. She gives him twenty-five bucks a week for sometimes taking out the trash. He has a nine-foot Nintendo screen in the bathroom and a wet bar in his closet. I don't have any of that. All I've got is a mom like you—strict, old-fashioned, don't let me get away with much—and I'm grateful.

If your son agreed with your discipline, would he really need a parent?

"You know what else I realized? You're not trying to be mean. You're trying to teach me self-control, and that will help me when I'm grown up. So if it's all right with you, I'm going to finish my homework and go to bed early, after I write letters of apology to all the family members."

Have you heard this? You'd better check that kid's temperature; he's getting delirious.

If your son agreed with your discipline, if he learned quickly, would he really need a parent? He could probably get by with a consultant who showed up every few months with some recommendations, and he'd take it from there.

On the first day of first grade, you could say, "Newton, before you get on the bus, let me tell you something. Son, do your arithmetic homework every day for the next twelve years. You don't know what you'll want to be twelve years from now, so keep all your options open, OK?"

And he'd respond, "Why, thank you, Mother. That makes such sense. I'm surprised they never mentioned it in preschool." And you'd never have to monitor his arithmetic homework again.

As much as we grown-ups talk about the importance of owning up to our actions, we don't like being disciplined either. We too will do whatever we can to avoid it.

Have you ever been stopped by a state trooper? "Ma'am, I clocked you at seventy-one miles an hour." And you said, "Oh, no, Officer, I was doing at least seventy-six. And yes, you caught me today, but I've been speeding through here every day on my way to work for the past three years. I should owe the state some back money for that."

It is the nature of the being, young or old, to avoid unpleasant consequences and thus to learn things the long way.

Disciplining for Success

Dear Dr. Ray,

I know discipline needs to be consistent to work best, but it seems I'm on my kids all the time, and I'm not seeing much improvement.

Constance

A core truth of good parenting: good discipline will bring great results, given enough time. The key word here is *time,* best defined in years, not weeks or months.

This truth is why the best of parents can get discouraged and frustrated. The results you want often come with the speed of a glacier, not a flash flood. What's more, as is so with much of parenting, the hard truths about kids are even harder for us grown-up types. As slow as we think the kids are to learn, our rate of maturation is more snail-like. Focus on this next time you're wondering, "Are they ever going to get this?"

Putting discipline in a realistic time frame will lessen your exasperation; it won't cure it. Sometimes parents feel as if they are on their kids because they *are* on their kids. We confuse real discipline with words and emotions. Nagging, negotiating, pleading, threatening, yelling, chastising, lecturing—all are illusions of discipline. They may sound like discipline, feel like discipline, even get cooperation here and there, but they are *not* discipline. More and more of these measures are needed over time to get the same results.

Real discipline leads to less discipline over time. Illusory discipline leads to more illusory discipline over time.

Thus a self-perpetuating pattern evolves. Ninety-seven percent of what we are doing is fueling our feelings of futility because 97 percent of what we are doing is futile. It is mostly verbal clutter and emotional turbulence. Only a small part of what is happening is real discipline—

limits enforced by consequences. Real discipline leads to less discipline over time. Illusory discipline leads to more illusory discipline over time.

To get an estimate of your consistency level, try this exercise. (Brace yourself; the numbers may not be pretty.) Consider your most challenging child, the one who pushes hardest, resists most and frustrates your best parenting efforts. Think of the neighbor kid if you have to. The experts variously would tag this child oppositional, strong-willed or difficult. Most likely he or she is just a kid who's feistier by nature than his or her siblings.

On average, how many times a day does this child get disciplined—that is, the child experiences an actual consequence: heads for his or her room, is fined for neglecting a chore, writes an apology, goes to bed early, loses a privilege? Most parents answer anywhere between zero and two times. Those with true Spikes and Spikettes may reach three or four.

The second question: On average, how many times a day does this child ignore you, defy you, throw a fit, torment a sibling, break a house rule, badger you, slough responsibilities? In other words, how many times a day does he or she misbehave, as you define it? Many parents respond with some version of, "Do you want it to the nearest hundred?" or, "The numbers aren't too high at night, when she's asleep," or, "Let me get my calculator; it goes up to six figures."

After we get down to brass numbers, most totals fall between twenty and fifty. Indeed, twenty is not all that much. If a child is home all day, twenty breaks down to about two incidents per waking hour.

Now take the actual discipline daily average—let's use the high number, say two—and divide that by the lowest misbehavior number, say twenty. Answer: ten percent. That is the discipline consistency level, the percentage of time that an actual consequence follows misbehavior. Scary, isn't it?

Of course, I don't know what your personal consistency numbers are. If you feel as if you're on the kids constantly, your words may be replacing action, and your consistency ratio will be low.

Sometimes discipline takes a long time to work because we take a long time to discipline. Hunter has been stalking his sister Harmony for the better, or should I say worse, part of an hour. Variously we've ignored, reasoned and warned, thereby grasping a few seconds of intermittent peace for Harmony and us. Nothing we've tried has brought lasting peace (with kids, "lasting" means twelve minutes or more). Finally we act: "Hunter, you will be your sister's servant for the next hour because you tormented her for an hour." (I tell my kids that this discipline is good preparation for marriage.)

Now, in fact, you did discipline, but also, in fact, you waited for nearly an hour. Likely there were dozens of individual bits of misbehavior that went undisciplined during that time. So while Hunter paid the price for his actions in the end, he played almost the whole game for free. For discipline to work well, it must be not only real but timely. The longer we wait to discipline, the longer we'll wait to see success.

There is good news and there is bad news. First the bad news: The best of discipline with the best of consistency and the best of timing takes much longer to shape character than most of us realize. The good news: What is more crucial than shaping character?

Discipline Discord

Dear Dr. Ray,

My wife and I don't always agree on how to discipline our son and daughter. She says I can be too hard on them. I think she gives in too much.

Disunited Front

Parents who don't see eye-to-eye always on discipline are the rule rather than the exception. Two people typically don't concur on something as limited as clothing preference. Can we expect them always to agree on something as complex and ever-evolving as child rearing?

Two people not being of one discipline mind is not in itself a deterrent to good parenting. Nor is it necessarily psychological trouble for your children. Its main complication comes from giving the kids opportunities to play Mom against Dad while standing by, gauging the direction of the sparks and aligning themselves with the victor. The victor, in kid parlance, is the parent who sees things their way.

Nobody really wins when one parent challenges the other in a child's presence. Even if the dissenting parent's discipline is more fitting or "correct"—if there is such a thing—he or she risks other problems, such as unwittingly sending the message that Mom and Dad will wrangle until bad feelings overshadow everything or until any fair discipline unravels in the ensuing heat. If Darrow can get the folks to bicker over his behavior, I'm sure he'll save some of his best testiness for when both are around. If nothing else, during the confusion he'll be able to slip away.

This is not to say that parents should never disagree within child earshot. Sometimes you both may feel that some discipline is needed, and your give-and-take is just a fine-tuning of your approach. The key is not to undercut each other.

One way to live on more common discipline ground is to agree to talk over incidents or problems after they occur. Put another way, you are agreeing to disagree, later in private, in exchange for public silence at discipline time.

Further, if after consideration you decide to tone down your initial discipline, you will apologize to the kids. You are not apologizing for the discipline; you are apologizing for overdoing it. A genuine apology for overreacting enhances discipline credibility. If nothing else, it shocks the kids into rethinking their image of you as the rock that never budges.

No matter how conscientiously you and your wife work to smooth out differences, some will remain. No two parents have the same personality. You are distinct in patience, tolerance level, voice volume, consistency and wordiness, among other things. All this translates directly into parenting differences. And that's not all bad. It adds to the richness of family life. At the least it keeps it exciting.

Ongoing discussion is a good long-term solution to discipline discord. A more immediate path to reduced discipline discord is house rules. These are simple expectations backed by simple consequences. For maximum success a house rule needs several features:

1. Most importantly, both parents must agree on it. Without mutual support a house rule becomes merely another point of child-rearing contention.

2. A house rule involves a recurrent (weekly, daily, hourly, minutely) trouble spot, such as back talk, sibling quibbling, chore shirking, temper tempests. It is best used for the most irritating stuff.

    The good Lord gave the whole world ten core rules. A house is a much smaller place.

3. House rule consequences are automatic. They result when the rule is broken, without nagging (I'm telling you one last time, Butkus, I don't want to have to call in our rule), re-reminding (What did I say was the new rule? Do you remember? Do you want me to write it on your arm?) or threatening (OK, break the rule one more time, and see if what happens.). Let your consequences do your talking.

4. Try to keep your rules to a manageable number. The good Lord gave the whole world ten core rules. A house is a much smaller place.

House rules provide the common ground upon which you and your spouse can stand. With agreed consequences in place, neither of you has to judge what to do each and every time the kids act up. Besides making expectations clearer for the kids, rules make discipline less open-ended for parents.

Here is a sampler of house rules:

- *You fight, you write.* Each party writes a 250-word apology to the other or others.

- *You talk back, you walk back*, or *You get mean, you leave the scene.* Back talk leads to an immediate half hour or more in a room alone, if logistics permit. If not, delay the room stay until it is possible. Time doesn't count unless it's quiet. For good measure, add a two-hundred-word report on a topic of choice from the encyclopedia. Who knows, someday they could become Jeopardy champions.

- *Pick up or pay up.* Every item Mom or Dad has to pick up goes in a box (bag, closet, warehouse) for one week. Fifty-cent fee for return.

- *You shirk, you work.* If you neglect doing your household chore on time, privileges are unavailable until that chore and an additional one are complete.

Rules are kind discipline for all parties. For kids they quietly lay out expectations. Less arguments, harsh words and hurt feelings ensue when guidelines are clear. For parents rules bring peace. In place prior to trouble, they are a means for order, harmony and thus a genuinely united front.

FOUR

Respect Yourself—and Me

Take a survey. Ask a hundred parents of teens: What is the number one daily discipline struggle with your teenager? The survey will say, respect. Parents describe the problem with thesaurus-like variety: attitude, lip, moodiness, mouth, snot. (There's an irony here in using so many facial terms to describe an age so focused on appearance.)

The words vary, but the essence is the same. Something about these adolescent years seems to breed automatically a surge in surliness. Is it an expected part of growing up—an immature passage to maturity, if you will? Is it something parents just have to weather until the kids become semihuman again? Should you just be grateful they're not doing anything worse during these turbulent years?

My comeback to each of these questions? *Yeah, right. Like no way.*

Battered Parent Syndrome

Dear Dr. Ray,

I'm a grandfather many times over. I'm shocked at how some of my grandkids talk so disrespectfully to their parents. Sometimes the parents don't even seem to notice.

My Father Noticed

I call it the "Battered Parent Syndrome." Mom or Dad has allowed verbal misconduct for so long that she or he has become nearly oblivious to it. The snotty tone, mean comebacks and disdainful looks are now such a standard feature of the parent-child interchange that most are ceasing to register. A typical scenario might unfold something like this:

Child: Mom, are you ready to leave yet? Why are you taking so long? We've been here for an hour. I want to go.

Mom: I know, Honey. I'm sorry. I'm almost done. Let me finish my coffee, and then we'll go.

Child: You said that fifteen minutes ago. If I had known you were going to take this long, I wouldn't have come. Let's go now, not fifteen minutes from now.

Mom: OK. Please just give me a few more minutes to tie up some loose ends. I'll tell Grandpa good-bye, and then I'll be all ready to leave.

Child: Just give me the keys. Give me the keys. I'll be in the car waiting. Hurry up.

This child is blistering her mother verbally while mom is talking accommodation and singing "Kumbaya."

Some parents might accept such surliness as the cost of letting Sabrina express herself. More often it appears to me that Mom or Dad has habituated to being the target of nastiness.

This child is blistering her mother verbally while mom is talking accommodation and singing "Kumbaya."

Sometimes when I get parents in my office with a teen, I try to raise their level of awareness of that disrespect. They know something is wrong, but they can't put their finger on what it is. Further, my telling them would be a distressing revelation. So I ask clients, "Do you hear how he is talking to you? Do you want to be treated that way?"

Now, if you're tempted to comment to your children or in-laws about what you're hearing, be careful. They are not just unaware; they may be defensive. After all, you're pointing out a "flaw" in their parenting. I can get away with pointing out such dynamics better than you can because (1) I'm not a relative, and (2) I'm getting paid to give feedback. Though sometimes folks don't take it well coming from me either.

Sometimes the reaction is a stunned one, as if the parent is being slapped awake. The look says, "Hey, you're right. I am getting mistreated, aren't I?"

Sometimes the reaction is one of embarrassment. The parent realizes that somebody else clearly has noticed what he or she has been permitting, however unintentionally.

An even less threatening way to raise your children's consciousness is to speak directly to their children. "Do you hear how you're talking to your father?" Or, "Is that how you speak to your mother?" In reality these are rhetorical queries meant for your own children's ears. If your grandchildren were to actually answer you honestly, they might admit, "Yeah, I do," and, "Yes, it is." Of course, if they were so bold, I think the shock effect on your children and in-laws would do more for opening their eyes and ears than anything you could ever say.

One more suggestion, this one for you parents still raising kids. If you're wondering how self-aware you are, ask yourself, "How would I react to another adult if he or she treated me the way my child is treating me?" If the answer is, "I'd thank him for being so open and authentic with his feelings," or, "I'd feel flattered that he is so comfortable in our relationship," then at least you're consistent. You like having everybody—young or old—talk to you poorly.

If your answer is, "I wouldn't like it one bit," then use this realization to begin taking action. Mistreatment isn't any less mistreatment because it comes from someone much younger than you. Upon recognizing what has been evolving for some time, the parent can at least consider how to reverse the process.

Cutting Back on Back Talk

Dear Dr. Ray,

I have three teenagers, all with distinct personalities. One thing they all have in common, though, is back talk.

Never the Last Word

Back talk: the universal teen misbehavior. Wherever they are there it is—unless, of course, your children absolutely never need limits or discipline. Maybe yours just naturally go to bed before the birds wake up, eat supper with and talk to the family and put their shoes away before the smoke alarm goes off.

Basic back talk comes in two types: grumble talk and nasty talk. Grumble talk is clearly the more benign. It is essentially Polly's editorial comment about the way you're raising her or running the house: "I'm just a slave around here." "How'd you keep the house clean before I was born?" "This is the fourth time this week I've had to hang up my coat." "You'd never let me look at you like that; how come he gets away with it?"

Grumble talk may not be disrespectful. It's often more of a whiny, maybe feebly, provocative attempt to pull you into an argument. Since it takes two to tangle, if you don't react to it, most grumble talk will die out from lack of fuel. Quietly shrug off Polly's complaining, so long as she is hanging up her coat for the fourth time this week or is doing the slavish work you ask of her.

Sometimes what can you really say? Fill the dog's water bowl again? How can you drive her so hard? Maybe she *is* the only ninth-grader in school who has to do her homework before she does her nails.

Sometimes you can defuse grumble talk by agreeing with it. For instance: "This is the third time I've taken out the garbage this week." "True." Or, "I always have to make my bed." "Yes, you do." No sarcasm from you. Just a matter-of-fact acknowledgment that what

Harmony is grumbling about is the way it is. With you agreeing, there's nobody left for Harmony to grumble to.

Teens are also masters of the mumble grumble. The technique is straightforward: Turn your back on Mom and walk away muttering discontentedly under your breath, just loud enough to let her know something is being said but just soft enough so she can't make it out.

Your instinctive response to mumble grumble might be to demand, "What did you say?" More than likely you'll receive the likes of, "I didn't say anything," or, "Can't a guy even talk to himself around here?" But you know he's talking to you; he never talks to himself in that tone of voice.

Here you have two choices. One, you can pretend you didn't hear at all what you couldn't quite hear, using the "prodigal son's brother" principle: if he's doing what you've asked, he's allowed to be unhappy about it. Or two, you can place a price on mumble grumble. Some prices are listed below under ways to deal with nasty talk.

Grumble talk typically doesn't escalate into verbal warfare if you can develop the attitude that "you can express your opinion as long as it's not disrespectful or nasty and as long as you meet your responsibility." In other words, if Polly is doing what you ask, you can't expect her always to be happy about it.

Whereas grumble talk generally can be soothed with little response, nasty talk requires action. Nasty talk is abusive or at least disrespectful, and it directly challenges your right and authority: "Don't tell me what to do." "You're stupid if you think I'm going to do that." "Get off my back." "I don't have to listen to you; just shut up."

One good way to discriminate between nasty talk and grumble talk is to ask yourself, "How would I react to this if it came from another adult?"

One good way to discriminate between nasty talk and grumble talk is to ask yourself, "How would I react to this if it came from another adult?" Nasty talk is talk that doesn't keep people friends very long.

Nasty talk is not expressing feelings; it is verbal meanness. And the younger a child is when he learns to control it, the better for him and others. All kids misbehave. But nasty talk, if left uncurbed, feeds on itself and can become a chronic challenge to your right to discipline in your child's best interests.

Nasty talk is talk that needs strong consequences. Here are some ideas. Very important point: These are linked to each instance of nasty talk.

1. Compose an essay on self-control, respect for others, expressing feelings appropriately and so on. The topic and length are the parent's choice. The parent can review the essay with the child, correcting for grammar and discussing content.

2. Look up, define and use in a sentence ten dictionary words (three syllables or more, not *a, an* or *the*). Keep a dictionary handy—say, near the kitchen table. If you have a particularly tough-talking teen, you may need a dictionary in every room. This approach was one mother's favorite. Her attitude was, "If you have to talk like that, you need a better vocabulary." By the time her son was fourteen, he had the highest vocabulary scores in his high school.

3. Use the dictionary creatively. Find and define ten words with a *z* in the middle. Or define fifteen words ending in *ion*. To play with Oxford's head a little, you could threaten, "You can't leave the kitchen table until you find ten words that begin with *qx*."

4. Levy a monetary fine for nasty talk. Teenagers may like to talk poorly, but they don't like to be poor.

The reverse of nasty talk is respect. What privileges can your teen earn by exercising self-control for, say, two days? Gradually lengthen the time required to earn perks such as extended curfew or phone time. Ask your teen what she'd like to earn. The request has to be within reason, of course. Otherwise you could hear, "An unchaperoned trip to Daytona Beach."

Lastly, remember that what is nasty talk is your judgment, not Gabby's. Debate it with her, and she'll give you that look that says, "What? I didn't say anything. What tone of voice? My lips never moved."

A Bad Age

Dear Dr. Ray,

My kids (ages eleven and fourteen) seldom get blatantly disrespectful, but they are giving me more subtle comebacks: eye rolls; half-joking "duh's"; "Yeah, right, Mom." My friends tell me, "Just let it pass; it's the age."

Yeah, I Am Right

I agree. It's the age—not the age of adolescence, as your friends think, but the age of toleration of disrespect that we now live in.

Sometimes I will tease a client: "What would your mother have done had you given her the attitude your son (or daughter) gives you?"

"Oh, I never would have done this stuff to my mother."

"Why? You were thirteen years old once. If teens are so automatically developmentally obnoxious, why weren't you?"

"Well, I may have felt like it, but I didn't do it. I just knew something bad would happen."

"What?"

"I don't know."

"Why didn't you know?"

"Because I never did it."

"Why didn't you do it?"

"I knew something bad would happen."

"What?"

"I don't know."

And on it goes, like an Abbot and Costello routine. But do you see the reality it speaks of? Our parents demanded respect—verbal and nonverbal—and we knew it and acted—and looked—accordingly.

Your children's subtle disrespect—though no disrespect is subtle if you can perceive it—puts a face on a broader mentality that undercuts good parents today and ultimately hurts kids. I call it the "He's not on drugs" mentality. Because what the child is doing is not all that bad, a parent needs to be more accepting of—perhaps even grateful for—the little misconduct, the normal stuff of kids. Because some problems are typical, they will resolve with time. So goes the reasoning.

Such reasoning totally ignores the core question of parenthood: What kind of person do I wish to raise? For the most part a parent can raise kids who are "not on drugs" by holding to culturally average standards. To raise a child of exceptional virtue and character, however, almost always requires adhering to standards well above the group norm. So the question for really good parents is not, is this behavior all that bad? The question is, is this behavior all that good?

Your friends are right in one sense. As kids get older, they become ever more skilled at walking a fine line between expressing themselves and disrespect. Four-year-olds have little finesse. When they're mad at us, the whole world knows. Fourteen-year-olds can be so smooth that it's an hour after the fact when we finally realize, "Hey, I was put down."

The question for really good parents is not, is this behavior all that bad? The question is, is this behavior all that good?

To determine whether or not it's wise to tolerate your youngsters' disparaging looks and covert commentary, try this test. For the next month, whatever your kids do to you, do the exact same thing to your best friend, your boss or your pastor. So anytime someone says or does anything you disagree with or don't like, simply respond, "Well, duh!" or "Yeah, right" or the ubiquitous "Whatever." At the end of the month, ask them, "Do you like the new me?" See if they reply,

"Well, you're not on drugs. And I do love the way you are so open with your authentic self. I never have to wonder what you're thinking." Yeah, right.

You see, when removed from the context of "that's just what kids do," the more harmless stuff doesn't seem so harmless. Certainly kids misbehave in lots of ways, big and small, because they're incompletely socialized human beings—aren't we all, really?—but that does not make small misconduct either acceptable or right.

I can imagine myself standing before a judge for some civil infraction and saying, "Come on, Your Honor, you get all kinds of big stuff in here: murder, robbery, arson. I don't do any of that. It's not like I'm a criminal or anything."

While eye rolling isn't in the same league as joint rolling, is it wrong or isn't it? The parent who says, "No, I don't think it is," doesn't need to do anything about it. The parent who sees it as wrong, though minor, does.

Respect is a package. It has verbal and nonverbal components. To reduce your teens' snotitude, try a zero tolerance approach. Permit none of it, which means, put a price tag on it. How about one hour of labor per look? a hundred push-ups per eye roll? look up, define and use in a sentence ten synonyms for each "whatever"? a picture of you as a teenager in your son's room for every dirty look?

Surly attitude quickly becomes a habit, taking on a life of its own. And the little stuff lays the base of temptation to use the bigger stuff. Stop it all. You'll feel a whole lot better, and your kids will be a whole lot nicer.

You don't agree? Oh, puh-lease, get real.

Addenda

Dear Dr. Ray,

I have to get firm and say, "I mean it!" or, "Now!" to get my kids to listen. And they're starting to ignore me even then.

Help. I Mean It.

It sounds as if your kids have trained you to resort to what I call addenda. It's a sticky trap that can pull in even the best of parents.

What are addenda? They are words or sentences tacked on to a parental request or command, designed to add weight to the original words.

Here are my top seven parental addenda: 1) I mean it! 2) Did you hear me? 3) Now! 4) I'm not going to say it again! 5) I said (then repeat original directive). 6) Don't make me come over there! 7) First, middle, last name (varies from child to child).

What's the problem with using addenda anyway? First, as you are finding out, they don't work. In the beginning they grab some attention or compliance, but their power fades with time.

Second, they convey a false message. Do you only mean it when you say, "I mean it"? If you don't say it, does that mean you don't mean it and, in fact, you are just talking to hear yourself talk?

Do you only mean it when you say, "I mean it"?

Third, addenda tend to get loud. The more they are used, the easier they are to fire off with increasing volume. And it's a short step from high decibels to high emotions. After a while that can take its toll on both you and little Adler.

Last and most important, when it comes to discipline, the persuasive power of words isn't improved with more words. If a twelve-word request wasn't heeded, why would a fifteen-word one be? A truism of discipline is that the teaching power lies in the consequences, not the words. Addenda are attempts to add weight to words that have lost their weight.

So how do you withdraw from addenda? It's probably best to go cold turkey. Stop using them. What can you put in their place to give yourself more authority with your kids?

There is one kind of addenda that works pretty well. Here are examples: "Hazel, please pick up the family room." Addendum: "If I ask you again, you'll vacuum it too." "Butkus, leave your brother alone." Addendum: "Or you'll head for your room for half an hour." "Don't nag me, Constance." Addendum: "The next time you ask, the answer is automatically no."

Action addenda work; word addenda don't, not long-term anyway. Authority comes from consistently meaning what you say. And meaning what you say comes from backing your words with consequences, not more words.

So don't do it anymore, OK? I mean it. I'm not writing just to watch myself write. Do you read me?

From Slander to Libel

Dear Dr. Ray,

I make my older kids write essays of apology if they are disrespectful. But sometimes the essays are nastier than the original nastiness.

Déjà Vu

Do you worry that what originally looked to be pretty creative and suitable discipline is backfiring? Rather than prompting Agatha and Christie to ponder thoughtfully the nature of their conduct, are you provoking them to more wrath? Instead of teaching respect, are you fueling more disrespect? Would it be better to forego the essay and not provide a forum for more venting?

A core law of parenthood: No matter how creative your discipline, a child can find a way to outmaneuver it.

I've always been fascinated by the tone of the typical parent magazine article, which assumes that if only you properly discipline Harmony, she will understand, accept and be grateful. No arguments, no resistance, no escalation, just full cooperation. I love fantasy.

Sometimes an essay is just a written fit. When youngsters don't agree with what you're doing as a parent—and such is the case with most discipline—they usually let you know somehow. Don't abandon a good discipline idea because your kids try to turn it against you. Their ploys don't mean the idea is bad; most likely they mean just the reverse. Your kids are driven to convince you to abandon your approach, as it is having an effect.

A great thing about being a parent is that you don't have to outthink the kids. You own the game. Make a few rule changes:

1. Respect is expected, whether verbal or written. So essay nastiness not only invalidates the original essay but leads to a second one.

2. Disrespect within the essay nullifies the whole essay, not just the offensive parts. Otherwise, savvy kids will just expunge the offending sections and recycle the sections that bespeak what a truly remarkable parent you are to have raised such fine offspring.

3. A consequence of a different sort, in addition to the essay, may be added. For instance, a mean screed leads also to one hour's worth of labor. After all, most verbal disrespect is impulsive or emotional or a bad reaction to your bad reaction. Written disrespect is more calculated and deliberate, usually representing a premeditated commentary on your parenthood. Thus it may need additional discipline.

Almost all discipline works through repetition. Because Edgar Allen reacts poorly to his first twenty essays in no way means he won't learn some valuable self-control, even virtue, from essays number twenty-one through infinity.

Sometimes an essay is just a written fit. Hey, it's better than having stuff thrown at your walls.

I Say, You Say

Dear Dr. Ray,

No matter what I say, my son always has a comeback. What do you do with kids who always have to have the last word?

Next to Last

It depends on what the last word is. Is it, "Gosh, Mom, you always make so much sense"? Or, "Most certainly I'll finish my homework before I rake the leaves"? How about, "Sometimes I honestly do feel like arguing with you, Mother, but I know you'll win because you're so much wiser about life than I am"?

If your son's retorts are anything like these, I would (a) kiss him, (b) nominate him for PTA poster boy, (c) bring him out in public as much as possible or (d) have him assessed psychiatrically.

Because I have heard a lament similar to yours from hundreds of parents, I'm going to take a wild guess and assume that you are not hearing any of the above. Rather, your son is arguing with you, challenging your rules and requirements, debating your decisions. In essence, his "comebacks" occur only when you ask or tell him anything he finds disagreeable. Am I on safe ground?

To begin, the number of your son's comebacks is directly related to the number of your comebacks. Put another way, he'll argue as long as you do. What does he have to lose? He's counting on any one of several things to happen: (1) you'll change your mind (primary goal),

(2) you'll collapse from the weight of the words (secondary goal), (3) you'll stand your ground but only after paying a heavy verbal and emotional price ("salvage something" goal).

The number of your son's comebacks is directly related to the number of your comebacks.

As long as you allow Sherlock to dictate the direction of the dialogue, he will become only more relentless. You need to add an outcome that Sherlock hasn't experienced consistently yet: arguing will gain him nothing; in fact, it will cost him.

Suppose you've just said, "Sherlock, be home by 7:00 PM." That's really all you need to say. He knows why: for supper, schoolwork, a family outing, whatever. He's lived with you for years. You've explained yourself and your motives for years. Seldom do you need to elaborate. Nevertheless Sherlock rebuts, "Why do I have to come home at 7:00? I don't want to go to Aunt Clara's."

Whatever you say next to explain further is pretty much irrelevant because it will elicit the same response from Sherlock: more debate. The word spiral spins a while longer until one or both of you really get mad, one of you gives in (guess who?), or one of you goes to Aunt Clara's but is miserable about it (guess who?).

Stopping this cycle falls on you. Why? Because you're the parent, for one, and because Sherlock likes things just as they are, for another. What are your options then?

You could simply cease talking and walk away. You've made your request; you don't want to fight about it. You could give Sherlock a look that says, "You'd better think real carefully about what you're about to say, because you're on thin ice."

(Have you noticed that sometime between the previous parenting generation and this one, the "look" has been lost? It seems to me that parents of the past were much more able to give looks that spoke volumes.

Not much in the way of endless words, warnings and threats needed to be uttered, for once Mom or Dad gave you that look, you knew you'd better back off because the next step would be consequential, to say the least.)

If you wish to do more than look, you might say, "Sherlock, one more word and you're in your room," or, "you'll be grounded for the next forty-eight hours," or, "you'll owe me fifty cents." In essence, instead of getting pulled into Sherlock's web of words, you'll be redirecting the dialogue: "Don't say any more or else."

Why do kids argue so much? Because they want to and because they're allowed.

Are they truly interested in understanding your ways? If they were, wouldn't you think that at least once or twice in the past decade, after twenty-seven minutes of nonstop negotiating, Sherlock would look up at you enlightened and confess, "You know, Mom, I don't always agree with the way you parent me, but if we bicker long enough, things do become so much clearer for me. Thanks, Mom, for taking the time to argue."

Express Yourself

Dear Dr. Ray,

If my son tells me one more time, "You just like things your way," whenever I say "No," I'll scream. I've let it go on because I've always felt he was expressing his feelings, but this is getting old.

Feeling Battered

A child-rearing notion that badly undercuts parents today says that, in the name of psychological correctness, we should allow children nearly unlimited license to express themselves. Much of what rightly was considered disrespect is now protected behind the shield of "venting feelings." Consequently, many parents fear squelching Miranda's opinions, however meanly meant and said, lest she become an emotionally pent-up, unhappy child. So erring on the safe side, they allow much that their head and guts tell them is pretty insulting stuff.

Much of what rightly was considered disrespect is now protected behind the shield of "venting feelings."

Certainly kids have a right to talk and be heard. But that right ends where disrespect and nastiness begin. For many parents the real struggle is where to draw the line separating positive openness from negative intent. A general suggestion: Feelings that are expressed with regard for others' feelings are allowed; those that batter another's feelings are not.

Many parents choose to ignore the standard kid gripes: "You don't like me," "I don't like you," "You like Harmony better," "You hate me," "You're unfair," "You're mean," "You're old-fashioned," "You're a parent" (I threw this one in because it's often what they're saying). Most of us will tolerate kid commentary of this ilk if it doesn't get too obstinate or repetitive. In other words, we don't like it, but we'll put up with it if they don't push too hard.

For you the repeated hammering is what's wearing. And your son probably knows or at least senses this. I sense that you want to stop him but believe it is beyond your parental discretion to stifle his freedom of speech.

In reality your son's First Amendment rights, like grown-ups', aren't limitless. He has gone beyond an occasional burst of opinion to a chronic insult. "You just like things your way" is ludicrous, but even a mildly irritating sentiment can become abusive if said with enough force or repetition.

An old propaganda adage says, "Repeat a lie often enough, and people will come to believe it." Your son is repeating a lie. Rather than getting his anger off his chest, he may be reinforcing in his mind what he says.

Follow your instincts. If you don't like this barrage, if you think it's offensive, stop it. You're allowed. Honest.

Words Without End

Dear Dr. Ray,

How can I keep my kids from nagging? They hammer away at me until I either cave in or lose my temper. And the more tired I get, the harder they push.

Nagging Fears

Nagging illustrates a great paradox of parenthood. The more parents nag, the less kids respond. The more kids nag, the more parents respond. Are they smarter than we are? Do they have more psychological stamina?

The reality is that if nagging didn't work, kids wouldn't do it. Kids realize this after a few years of life. Parents realize it after a few kids.

The art of nagging is elegantly simple: Use relentless words in pursuit of a goal. The short-term goal is to get what you want. The long-term goal is to soften Mom or Dad's resistance to future nagging.

Nagging illustrates a great paradox of parenthood. The more parents nag, the less kids respond. The more kids nag, the more parents respond.

Compared to parents, children are relatively powerless. They don't have control over their environments the way we do. So through words—millions of them—comes their power to persuade. Kids count on our ears tiring long before their vocal cords do.

There are two occasions when kids are more persistent than normal. (Normal persistence is considered five to ten nags per minute.) The first is when they *really, really* want something, as opposed to the much less urgent *really* want something.

Let's say you are considering granting Desiree a special treat or privilege. She can't chance that you'll make a decision based solely upon its merits, so she dramatically kicks up her level of pleading, begging and overall obnoxiousness. A good way to short-circuit this verbal jackhammering is to say, "Don't ask again, even once, or the answer will be 'No.' I need quiet to think."

To break nagging's grip, you must not let it work. That's easy for me to write. I'm in my office listening to a radio I can unplug if I want. Kids don't have "off" buttons.

If you feel you can reach deep within and tap an unused reservoir of resolve, you could practice ignoring all nagging words. After you've said no to "Mom, can I ride the triple-spiral demon a seventeenth time?" act as though Constance is no longer speaking. In time—anywhere between a minute and a decade—she will wind down.

If you're like most of us parents and doubt your ability to stay oblivious for thousands of words at a time, or if you simply don't want to hear it, you could implement a gag order: "Tucker, if you nag, you will nag in your room," or, "you will write fifty times, 'Nagging is not a good way to communicate.'" Would fifty times constitute written nagging?

One mother simply asked, "Are you nagging?" She really was saying, "Don't nag, or there will be consequences." The kids knew the consequences. They'd earned them a few dozen times before "Are you nagging?" was sufficient to silence them.

Once kids realize that you will not be verbally browbeaten, they will look for other ways to get what they want. That's good, I think.

So I hope you'll try these suggestions. OK? Just for a few weeks. See if they work. All right? Just a couple of them. Promise? You asked the question, so you can at least consider the answer. C'mon. What've you got to lose? Are you listening to me?

Wait Until Someone Gets Home

Dear Dr. Ray,

I'm a grandmother. Many in my generation heard, "Wait until your father gets home," if we misbehaved. Kids these days don't hear this very often. Good or bad, in your opinion?

Waiting

It depends. (Don't shrink-type answers just drive you crazy sometimes?)

First, let's look at why kids don't hear this once stock child-rearing phrase all that much anymore.

One, the dad-at-work, mom-at-home family arrangement is no longer typical. Indeed, only about 25 percent or so of modern families fit this profile. Therefore, reality simply doesn't permit as many kids to experience this venerable discipline warning. In fact, you'd think that with dual-employed parents as the norm, a few frustrated fathers somewhere might be threatening, "Wait until your mother gets home."

Two, even some stay-at-home moms never utter, "Wait until your father gets home." That's because in many families *the* authority is already home: Mom. More and more I'm hearing mothers lament that they set the rules for kids, while Dad is "Mr. Nice Guy" or "Disney Dad" or "Mr. Laid-Back." It's tough to count on strong backup from Dad when Mom is the strong one.

Three, experts—I always get nervous using that word—have stressed repeatedly that moms need authority equal to dads. They see it as bad parenting practice to rely on an unseen, future enforcer to give Mom some "real" discipline strength. It puts Dad in an unfair position while lowering Mom's status in kids' eyes.

For the most part I agree with this idea. A mother with personal authority benefits all members of the family. For herself she gains respect and better cooperation. Little kids particularly act better facing immediate rather than delayed discipline.

To her kids a strong mom gives predictability and security. They know she is willing to act *now* to keep the household running smoothly. It will not be turmoil for nine hours until the hammer comes down.

To her husband she gives peace. He doesn't walk in the door warily anticipating a litany of kid trouble to deal with, along with a frazzled spouse. Mom may be weary from the day's demands, but discipline edginess won't be part of it.

Where then is the "depends" part of my original answer to your question? In good families the separate authority of Mom and Dad is really one. Thus, if Harmony challenges Mom all day long, even though Mom dealt with her well, Dad may choose to deal with her when he arrives. His rationale? Harmony gave his wife grief, and Dad will augment Mom's discipline to teach a stronger lesson.

In good families the separate authority of Mom and Dad is really one.

When our children were younger, I learned to sense subtle clues that my wife had had a rough day. At times she would meet me halfway up the driveway, with two children in each arm, mumbling in Seussian rhyme, "I do not want them in my hair; I do not want them here or there. You'd better take them, Ray I am. For I am crazy, yes, I am."

From years of psychological training, I learned to recognize these early signs of overload. I also learned to add my fatherly authority to my wife's. Yes, she disciplined them on difficult days, and sometimes so did I. The children realized that their mother and I were together in this parenting journey. You rattle her; you rattle me.

Thus their mom seldom had to say, "Wait until your father comes home." They knew that when I came home, if Mom was rhyming, they were in big trouble.

FIVE

Trouble Trademarks of the Teens

Every stage of childhood comes with its own trademark misbehaviors. Preschoolers give us temper tempests, bedtime bad times, meal ordeals, toy litter, disrespect. Elementary aged kids are prone to sibling quibbling, tattling, homework hassles, disrespect. And from teens we get chore shirking, disrespect, curfew busting, disrespect, schoolwork avoidance, disrespect, …

We've given the matter of respect its own section in this book; it deserves it. Here we will tackle a few more trademark issues of the teen years.

Kids Don't Make Good Parents

Dear Dr. Ray,

My fourteen- and twelve-year-old sons bicker constantly, sometimes leading to all-out fights. I've read that I should let them resolve their own conflicts, but I'm afraid they'll hurt each other long before they learn to get along.

On the Sidelines

Would you allow your fourteen-year-old to set his brother's bedtime? How about his household duties? Would you let him decide what constitutes back talk and then apply discipline? Of course not. Why? Because he's not his brother's mother. And he has neither the maturity nor judgment to teach his brother how to live well.

The notion that siblings should learn to resolve their own conflicts while parents stay clear of the fray is a popular one among experts.

The hope is that kids will figure out eventually through constant jock-eying, sparring and free-for-alling how to get along. As long as parents don't "intrude" with their rules and expectations, children will teach themselves and therefore will more readily accept what they've learned.

Like most trendy "new and improved child rearing," this idea sounds good on paper. It sure would be nice if kids could figure out how to do some of this parenting stuff on their own. Indeed, *if* siblings are close in age and size, and *if* they truly want to get along, and *if* they don't kill each other first, and *if* your house can survive their assault, and *if* you can weather the chaos, then maybe Rocky and Bruno can negotiate some peace or at least an uneasy truce.

Alas, in the day-to-day world of parenting, paper ideas can get shredded by real kids. First, I would guess that your fourteen-year-old is bigger, stronger, smarter and overall just a tougher opponent than his younger brother. Why would he feel compelled to "work something out" that surrenders his rights and desires? Seeking to control is a drive that begins young. It's not likely that a dominant sibling will negotiate away his status.

Then too, do you want to passively stand by while the boys torment, name call, hit and in general mistreat each other in the name of conflict resolution? Not only will the "weaker" child routinely end up losing, but a whole lot of mutual meanness will be unleashed by both. Kids are wonderfully resilient and forgiving, but a relentless battering of words or fists can take its toll on the strongest of sibling bonds.

Unrestrained permission to settle differences can be a license for filial warfare.

Third, a parent's duty is to protect. When we allow brothers and sisters to blast their way to a solution—notice that I didn't say "resolution"—we give up our responsibility to shield them from hurt, especially that caused by family members. Unrestrained permission to settle differences can be a license for filial warfare.

As mother, you set the rules for negotiation. Conflict resolution can occur only within the context of your parameters: no hitting, no name calling, no head butting, no gouging, no soap in the eyes, whatever. In my experience kids are much quicker to work out their disagreements when they know the rules of the game. Of course, if they break the rules, there are consequences for you to enforce.

I am not suggesting that you jump in at every squeak and squabble. For the little stuff sometimes a simple "work it out peacefully or you both sit" can spur an attitude of cooperation. After all, the worst of enemies will ally themselves in the face of a common adversary.

Testing the Sibling Bond

Dear Dr. Ray,

Any words for dealing with a fifteen-year-old who is verbally demeaning to his two younger sisters (ages thirteen and nine), sometimes abusively so?

Hurting With Them

Yes. Stop him.

The sibling bond can be bent, twisted, hammered and still hold. But why allow it to be so tested? Because a relationship can survive a battering doesn't mean the battering is good for it. I might stagger up after a face-first fall down a flight of stairs, but the fall isn't healthy for me.

The sibling bond can be bent, twisted, hammered and still hold. But why allow it to be so tested?

Parents often permit some sibling-on-sibling maltreatment because others—experts, family, friends—opine that it is to be expected that siblings will argue, clash, even abuse one another. Indeed, some expert types posit that it is developmentally good for sibs to tangle, as they will learn much needed conflict resolution skills. I wonder if such experts were only children.

Put another way, many say, "Don't worry. While the sibling bond may take a real licking, in the end it'll keep on ticking." I say, "Such a licking usually only leads to a ticking off—of all parties."

A verbal licking is particularly hurtful coming from an older sibling. A big brother or sister enjoys a natural status in a littler one's eyes. He or she is seen as a grown-up or a role model or even a protector. This intimate relationship can be fractured by an older sibling's disdain of the "lesser beings" of the family.

Indeed, the damage done can be measured by telltale remarks from the younger ones: "He's such a jerk." "Make him leave me alone." "I really like it when he's not home." "Does he have to come along?" Sure, some of this stuff is said by almost all siblings at one time or another. But it's the number and emotion of such laments that reveal the degree of resentment.

What's worse, sometimes the older child's tormenting is aimed laser-like at the younger's most sensitive spot: appearance, intellect, grades, weight. This can take a toll on a brother's or sister's ego, confidence or emotions. Your girls need your protection, as they are unable or unwilling to protect themselves.

Let's also not overlook your son's well-being in all this. By being allowed to act hurtfully, he deprives himself of an invaluable family gift: a warm relationship with siblings. He also learns to be habitually nasty. That's not a quality anyone—not just a littler sister—likes.

So back to my first words: stop him. But your words alone won't slow him down. You need action, firm and certain. Levy a consequence commensurate with his meanness. If you believe your son is really nasty to his sisters—and you seem to believe that—make sure your discipline reflects this.

Examples: possibly a full-day loss of *all* privileges for any mistreatment; a five-hundred-word written apology, including why he's grateful to have sisters; doing all of a sister's chores for three days; writing twenty-five good things about his sister. On this last one, if he says, "There aren't twenty-five good things about her," you could say what one feisty mom said to her child, "Make them up; I do with your father."

Is your goal to stop mistreatment in its tracks or just to tone it down to "normal"? "Normal" still implies that some level of mistreatment is allowed. Is this what you wish to communicate to him and to his sisters?

In the short term you probably won't alter your son's attitude toward his sisters; that will take time. But you will alter his conduct. Your son won't give vent to his disdain so freely, and your daughters won't have to hear it.

This alone will help heal some of the fraying of the relationship. When a child isn't permitted to be nasty, he has two options left: either he ignores his siblings, or he acts nicer. Fortunately, most kids learn to be nicer. Call it the pull of the sibling bond.

To Fee or Not to Fee

Dear Dr. Ray,

My husband and I disagree over whether or not to give allowances to our two sons, ages twelve and fourteen. He says they live here, so they should not be paid for chores. I think allowances are a good idea. Your opinion?

Fee or Free

Being a psychologist and therefore by trade somewhat prone to compromise, my opinion on allowances is somewhere between yours and your husband's.

Because kids are part of the family—though the older ones may be embarrassed about it, especially in public—it's logical that they have certain fee-free family responsibilities. The house is everybody's, so its care is everybody's.

"Family chores" for your sons might include making their beds, hauling out the trash, setting the table, keeping their rooms fumigated—certainly not too much to ask for the myriad of benefits they receive free from you. Family chores teach kids that all work does not deserve recompense. Such is good preparation for spousehood.

Other responsibilities—washing dishes, cleaning house, weeding—might be targeted as "wage chores" leading to allowance money. Wage chores give kids the chance to learn to earn. Such is good preparation for adulthood.

All family work must be completed before the privilege of earning an allowance begins.

A key point: Family chores precede wage chores. In other words, all family work must be completed before the privilege of earning an allowance begins. Otherwise the kids will head for the money chores first, leaving the family duties to Mom and Pop, who are used to working around the house for free.

What's a good allowance figure? That depends upon you and what expenses your sons are responsible for. I would offer this general guideline: reflect the real world. Giving Forbes five dollars a week for feeding the goldfish and walking the trash to the end of the driveway on Tuesday is a very generous wage. Actually it's unreasonable. Translated into an hourly rate, it comes to $712.00. Even professional adult goldfish keepers don't earn near that; only psychologists do. Then again, dispensing one dollar a week for converting the garage to a family room and reseeding the lawn is near serf labor. Use your own good sense to decide what's fair and what you can afford.

Allowances are a multi-benefit package. One, they teach kids to delay gratification. Buck makes his bed Monday through Friday and has to wait for any money payoff on Saturday. That's equitable. Rarely in the adult work world does one get paid the instant he finishes a task.

Two, allowances help reduce financial friction. Parents who give little or no allowance, instead choosing to judge money requests individually, run the risk of constant cash clashes, as kids routinely think their needs (such as a designer ball bat, a twenty-seven-speed hair dryer) are more critical to their happiness than parents do.

A third benefit: allowances are sound financial leverage. If Buck's bed isn't made, part of his allowance can go from his pocket into yours. After all, you did his work, and since you belong to Local 172 of the Bed Makers Motherhood Union, you can charge prevailing wage scale.

Lastly, allowances teach priorities. They help Chase experience firsthand that money supply is limited, something he doesn't realize when Mom and Dad are the bank. Thus he's forced to choose which extravagance he can afford, the remote-controlled ball glove or the commando rocks.

Allowances can be used creatively. One mom of mouthing teens fined her kids for spewing any off-color words. She had a list of twenty-five-cent, fifty-cent and dollar words. If her kids were going to use cheap language, it was going to cost them.

A Parent's Prerogative

Dear Dr. Ray,

Most of my fourteen-year-old son's friends receive far more allowance for far less work than he does. It's a source of chronic arguing between us. Do I need to reassess?

Stingy?

Of my three possible answers—yes, I don't know and no—I'll choose the latter two.

I don't know. Maybe you are giving your son a buck a month for painting the garage, making all his siblings' beds and remodeling the family room. If so, perhaps he does have merit to his case. On the other hand, if the discrepancy between your son's money-to-work ratio and his friends' is due to the fact that they are asked to do little or nothing to get paid a lot, then he has no case. Sadly, for you as well as your son's friends, this latter scenario is all too common.

Teens regularly base their whole argument upon one question: How can all those parents be wrong and you be right? Easy answer: They are and I am. Kids believe you should parent by consensus—if the consensus benefits them, that is. Your son never would bring to your mind any child in the Western Hemisphere who works harder for less than he does. No, that child's parent is even more lost than you are. And certainly your son never would point out where and how he has it better than the majority. Indeed, in such a rare event, in his eyes you *are* right and all those other parents *are* wrong.

My typical answer to questions like yours, in which a parent is second-guessing a decision because most others do it differently, is no, you don't need to reassess.

Most of the time your way is the right way because you have the right to determine what is right for you and your family.

First of all, in matters of morals and responsibility, I've observed that the majority doesn't provide high enough standards. Doubting yourself because others are lower in their expectations—or as your son might see it, more reasonable and fair—is generally not a good reason to rethink your standards or discipline.

Second, even if you are on the stingy end of the work-for-allowance continuum, so? If you took a poll of a hundred parents and only eleven agreed with you, so? (Am I sounding like a snotty sibling yet?) You are the parent; your child is not. That truth allots you great latitude in making whatever decisions you believe are best for your child. In essence, most of the time your way is the right way because you have the right to determine what is right for you and your family.

If you wish to give no allowance at all, I personally may not agree with you, nor perhaps would most other parents. Again, so? The question is not, are you being "psychologically correct" in your decision?

The question is, do you have the parental right to make that decision? And I acknowledge that you do.

Of course, parents can make terrible decisions. They can cling stubbornly to attitudes and practices that only hurt themselves and their kids. This is not my focus here. I am addressing the modern phenomenon of having good parents wonder if they are "allowed" to choose a parenting path that few are walking.

Yes, you are allowed, and yes, very often it's the better path. But you don't need me to agree with you on that.

Many Teens Make Light Work

Dear Dr. Ray,
Two teenagers, able-bodied, chore-resistant.

Working Alone

One psychologist, able-minded, chore-endorsing.

Once I asked a gathering of about fifty parents, "How many of you are getting the help you'd like around the house from your teens?" Three parents raised their hands. The others quickly called them show-offs or liars.

I asked the group, "If not, why not?" Survey results: 1) The kids' lives are so busy, not much time is left for chores. 2) We don't ask all that much. 3) The kids have outside jobs. And the number one reason: It's too much effort to get cooperation.

Many if not most small business owners will say their biggest obstacle to growth is finding good help, particularly young people with initiative, reliability and a solid work ethic. Such qualities don't develop automatically with age. They need a strong push during the growing years. So how do you push without getting tired yourself?

Since I myself run a small business—a family of twelve—I'll help you.

Set the schedule. How many rooms are in your home? How many kids? Divide the number of rooms by the number of kids (a husband can count as a kid, maybe two). Your answer is the number of rooms each person "owns." List on paper—discreetly placed inside a cupboard, on the back of a door, on a toilet seat, whatever—all that is involved in maintaining that room daily. What is your role? Though you can take a room or two, you are the supervisor, part of upper-level management.

How do you insure the rooms are cared for in a timely manner? Simple.

"Mom, can Heloise come over?" "Sure, if your rooms are done."

"Mom, will you iron my shirt?" "Of course, did you take out the trash for me yet?"

Privileges don't begin until responsibilities end. The goodies of teen life are not entitlements of age. They are privileges of the working class.

Jar the jobs. On small pieces of paper, write all your household jobs: vacuum dining room, clean toilets, sweep garage floor, clean out refrigerator, arrange closet, remodel family room, paint car, change transmission fluid. For misbehavior—disrespect, sibling quibbling, arguing, eye rolling, chore shirking—the job jar is the consequence. "Please reach in (blindly, of course) and grab a job." If your kids are going to be bad, at least your home will look real nice.

> **The goodies of teen life are not entitlements of age. They are privileges of the working class.**

Answer questions with questions. This is an old psychology trick. Examples:

"Mom, can I use the computer?" "Sure, is the family room picked up?"

"Will you take me to practice?" "I'd like to; will the dishes be done first?" (By the child, that is.)

"Can Sarah stay overnight Friday after skating?" "Can you clean the house? I wouldn't want Sarah to have to sleep in a messy place."

The typical teen has many requests of parents. Link those requests—however often you see fit—to helpful cooperation.

Adults routinely lament the stress of raising teens. Farmers of 150 years ago had the right idea: big kids = strong bodies = good help. A great advantage of having teens, particularly for moms, is the ready pool of domestic help. Ladies, as your kids grow, your days of hard, lonely labor should shrink.

A Kid's Room: No Place for a House

Dear Dr. Ray,

Any suggestions for getting kids to keep their rooms halfway livable? My children are eleven and fourteen, and their standard comeback is, "It's my room. Why can't I keep it the way I want?"

It's My House

Here are some parents' descriptions of their kids' rooms: "I'm afraid to go in there without a wilderness survival kit and an oxygen mask." "Two of her sisters accidentally stumbled into her bedroom about a year ago and were never seen again." "We call his room 'Star Trek': to venture in is to 'boldly go where no mom has gone before.'"

As creatively as parents can depict the messy room problem, so too can they relieve it. One mother said that, in a final fit of frustration, she gathered up all the debris decomposing on her son's floor and piled it on the bed; the mound hit the ceiling. Undaunted, her son slept on his newly discovered floor the next three nights. He finally did get the message and began to sort through the stack. Maybe he needed his sweatpants, buried somewhere near the bottom.

> **"We call his room 'Star Trek': to venture in is to 'boldly go where no mom has gone before.'"**

Another parent said that during a cleaning frenzy, he threw every item clogging up his son's bedroom out the front window. Upon returning from school, his son saw the shrubs wearing his gym shorts and T-shirts. To paraphrase an old saying, one picture is worth a thousand naggings. Things were borderline straightened after that.

Dramatic reactions like these can work, but they tend to be short-lived. After the fury has subsided, Comfort's room slowly returns to its pre-habitable state. Besides, the initial cleaning is done by the parent, not the child. More durable solutions to ruined rooms are available.

First, decide how you want to view your kids' rooms. (I know, from three miles away.) Parental philosophy here is divided into two camps. Some consider a youngster's room his domain: as long as the door is shut—ideally a steel-encased door with a twelve-inch external deadbolt—the room is out of sight and out of mind. Other parents believe, "It's her room, but it's my house, and I don't want part of my house below city health code."

Whichever philosophy you prefer determines what action you'll take. The "closed door" tact requires less effort. Basically the room just exists, and you count on Sandy to develop some desire eventually to keep his turf presentable. Sometimes this happens; other times it doesn't until a youngster has his own place.

In the latter case, here are added suggestions: do not enter the room to pick up clothes, bed sheets or other items that need your laundering, tailoring or general parental service. Sandy can 1) bring the clothes to the laundry room himself, 2) wash all washables himself, 3) repair and mend his own possessions. This is the price tag for keeping the room the way he wants it.

The "It's his room, but it's my house" mentality takes more of your energy, but it usually results in a better-kept room.

First step: Set up room inspection times, say 6:30 PM on Wednesday and 11:00 AM on Saturday. If conditions initially are too deplorable, you might want to set up daily or even hourly inspections.

Second step: Decide what the cost will be for a messy room. *Messy* is one of those loose terms that kids like to argue about, so maybe you'd best define *messy* or *unlivable* or *trashed*. What are some costs? Suggestions coming right up in the next "filthy room" question.

There's a bright side to the messy room situation. If you run out of storage space in your garage or shed, you can always park the lawn tractor in the room. The kid will never know it's there.

Good by Comparison

Dear Dr. Ray,

I have long been upset over the chronic condition of my fourteen-year-old's room. When my friend saw it, she laughed and said that I'm overreacting; I should see her son's room.

Calm Down and Lighten Up?

Why should you see her son's room? In your eyes your son's room is plenty gross enough. Bypassing for the moment the issue of how to get a clean room, let's analyze your friend's comments on several levels.

Level one: She says her son's room is less habitable than your son's. All that really tells us is that there are two rooms in your homes in a similar trashed state. While her son's may be objectively worse than yours, she is less displeased by it. That's her prerogative as a parent. It is irrelevant to whether or not your son's room should be acceptable to you. Your room standards very well may be different.

Level two: Should it give you solace that there are kids sloppier than yours? Any parent can find children more frustrating, defiant, rude, irresponsible, ungrateful or whatever than their own. So? All that says is that the harder you work to raise good human beings, the less other people will be like you. There is no comfort in comparing favorably to others if their standards are set lower. That's easy to do. The question is, how do you compare to your own standards?

Level three: Your friend is implying that your son is normal for his age, at least where rooms are concerned. That's true. The majority of teenage boys have rooms that would be condemned by local building codes. On one hand, that's good to know. It can keep you from reading too much into certain behavior. It is soothing to know that what Butler is doing is not atypical, bizarre or pathological. That can keep you from overreacting, as your friend says.

On the other hand, just because your son's conduct is normal doesn't mean it's good or desirable. What are acceptable room conditions among young boys may not be acceptable among mothers, who just happen to own the house that is built around the room. You have every right, even the responsibility, to set your standards where you wish, not just for your sake but also for your son's. You will teach him to cooperate with legitimate authority even when he does not agree with it. And that's a virtue that's getting less and less normal in our culture.

Level four: You need to relax and accept your son's room as is because he's not doing anything that bad, says your friend. Yes, in the overall scheme of parenting, disheveled rooms are down on most parents' priority lists. But again, in no way does this mean that you have to accept the room.

Maybe your friend was implying that you are getting too upset over this issue. That's possible, in which case you can tone down your words, nagging or emotions. But you don't have to tone down your expectations. It's one thing to work to better your discipline style. It's quite another to abandon your discipline altogether.

If the majority of parents' standards are slipping, then it is foolish to take the majority as a guide.

Level five, the most deeply destructive level: The message is that you should measure your parenting by others' parenting. Nowadays that's a sure path to raising a child quite unlike what you had hoped. If the majority of parents' standards are slipping, and I believe so, then it is foolish to take the majority as a guide. If all the other parents jump into the lake, are you going to jump in too?

Oh, I almost forgot. What about getting a cleaner room? Several ideas: 1) Send Dusty to his room periodically, and he can't come out until it's clean. 2) You clean it but charge him. And you're union, aren't you? 3) Take a large trash bag and sort through the debris. Of course, you can't know always what he does or doesn't want to keep. 4) Room inspection is Wednesday at 6:00 PM and Saturday at 10:00 AM. Not sufficiently tidied leads to an hour of extra chores, plus the cleaned room, before privileges begin.

I know what you're thinking. How did Dr. Ray get all those levels of interpretation from just a couple of statements? Remember, I'm a shrink. I'm practiced at overanalyzing. And I'm a parent. I'm practiced at overreacting.

Afraid of Commitment

Dear Dr. Ray,

How hard and long should a parent push a child to stay committed to an activity for which he has lost his initial enthusiasm?

Committed for Now

When I was twelve years old, my parents purchased an organ for my younger sister. "Me, too," I said. "I want to take lessons." Several lessons later, just about the time my interest in music was going flat, my teacher told my father, "He has a natural gift." The woman talked too much.

That convinced Pop; the man listened too much. His son would learn to play the organ. The months dragged on, and I was sure both my instructor and my father were singing the wrong tune. Regularly I argued with my dad, "It's not like I'm going to be a professional or something." Ah, the cocksure prophecy of youth.

Once past my initial period of resistance, and slowly gaining skill despite my worst efforts, this organ idea began to sound better. Some years later I turned professional ("or something"), and I entertained in restaurants for nearly a decade, earning enough money to leave college debt-free and having learned a skill for a lifetime. Had my father left the decision to me, I would have quit sometime in the first months, never knowing what I had denied myself.

How long and hard to insist a youngster maintain a commitment depends on many factors. A few:

Talent. How naturally is he gifted? It would seem that the better a youngster is at something, the longer he needs to allow it to make apparent its rewards.

Competition. Is Nielsen losing interest because other less worthy pursuits—such as television, computer games, phone—are more appealing? Kids are flooded with choices for leisure and time consumption. It is all too easy for junk to crowd out the worthwhile. Sometimes limiting the useless gives the useful more chance to take root.

Investment. How intense were Orville's initial pleading, pushing and persistence to take hang gliding? Was there a startup cost? Who paid? Who will pay if the activity is let go? Who else will be affected? Lefty may affect no one else if he quits origami class, but it's tough on a whole team to lose a pitcher midseason.

Pattern. Is this an isolated reaction or a style? Does Constance eventually lose interest in just about everything she tries? If so she may need to break a bad habit. If her resistance is out of character, give more credibility to her assurances that cliff diving is not for her.

> **"If you start you're in for one season or one year, whichever comes first. No escape clause."**

One mom told me of her rule of thumb: "If you start you're in for one season or one year, whichever comes first. No escape clause."

But what if the activity requires regular practice, and getting follow-through is taking more commitment from the parent than the child? How about giving Cliburn a choice: one half hour of practice can be replaced by one hour of chores? The only way to avoid practicing is by doing double time on work. Over a few months that should tell you how resistant is his resistance.

All of us try things that over time we find we don't like. The balance lies in spending enough time and effort to really find out that a particular pursuit is not for us, not so little that we prematurely conclude we're not for it.

Underachievement: School Problem Number 1

Dear Dr. Ray,

My son is fourteen years old. All his teachers say he is quite capable of doing his schoolwork, but his grades are very poor. He seems to lack initiative. What can I do to motivate him?

Tired of Pushing

Yours is by far the most frequent school-related question I receive from parents. In sheer numbers, underachievement—a child's not working up to potential—dwarfs the incidence of other, more highly publicized school problems such as school phobia and hyperactivity.

Before we try to motivate the under-motivated, one caution is needed. Some children who look like underachievers really aren't. Intellectual or learning problems underlie their school struggles temporarily. Likewise, life troubles can cause a child to push schoolwork into the background. These factors need to be ruled out through consultation with teachers or psychologists before concluding that a youngster is truly capable of more than he or she is showing.

Still, in the great majority of cases, kids who perform poorly in school are not hindered by learning or other problems. They are quite able to do their work, often at an above-average level. These are the youngsters whom we will talk about here.

Typically the underachievement pattern has been forming for several years. Resistance to schoolwork began back in the early grades, and motivation has continued to wax and wane ever since. Assignments regularly are not finished during class time. Homework routinely stays at school or is lost, left in the bushes, "forgotten," eaten by the dog or lied about. "Honest, Mom, this is the third teacher I've had since second grade who doesn't believe in homework or tests!"

The underachiever is the one to whom many parents refer when lamenting, "We've tried everything; nothing works."

The underachieving youngster seems to spend most of his scholastic energy finding ways to skirt schoolwork. Every so often an internal fire flares—usually during the early stages of some new system we're trying—but exasperatingly the fire is short-lived.

The underachieving child completely frustrates parents and teachers. He resists encouragement, rewards and punishment. Standard discipline is usually ineffective because little is powerful enough to overcome consistently this child's distaste for schoolwork. In short, the underachiever is the one to whom many parents refer when lamenting, "We've tried everything; nothing works."

What drives certain kids to be so undriven? Some downright dislike schoolwork. To them it is boring, frustrating or meaningless. They see little purpose in it and would much prefer occupying their school day with more immediately enjoyable pursuits, such as counting cars passing on the road outside, reassembling their pen each minute or watching their favorite daydreams playing on the ceiling.

Other children have subtle delays in such areas as maturity or concentration. Nothing is severe enough to warrant special services; overall these kids are still able to do the work. They just have to concentrate harder or spend a little more time at it. Consequently some of them take the initially easier route and gradually quit trying.

As seemingly stubborn a problem as underachievement is, it responds rather well to one particular approach. It's an approach that is elegantly simple and, perhaps more importantly, unbeatable. Even

Newton, as creative as he is, won't be able to find loopholes in it. Let's call it the note home procedure. Here's what to do:

Step 1. Obtain a small spiral notepad. This notepad will be your youngster's constant school companion. Require him to carry it to and from school every day. Actually any kind of record sheet will do. The advantage to a notepad is that it's small and holds a lot of pages, thus allowing you to look back to measure progress or see patterns.

Step 2. Keep a daily record. At the end of each school day or each period, if need be, Oxford is to list in his notepad all homework assignments, incomplete classwork, failed tests and anything else you would like included.

Step 3. Insure accuracy. In filling out his notepad, Oxford has the added responsibility of asking all teachers to initial it after class. Teachers give initials if *and only if* everything is listed correctly. If not they offer neither corrections nor initials. On any day that Oxford has finished all work at school, he writes "all work is done" and seeks the confirming initials.

Step 4. Schoolwork is completed immediately after school. Set up a quiet, isolated spot where all schoolwork can be finished. Only when schoolwork is completed correctly can privileges and activities begin, not until then. Schoolwork is the evening's first order of business.

Shouldn't Webster be given a "break" after school to unwind before beginning to work? I don't think so. He had his break at school. He didn't do much for six hours.

Step 5. The notepad is the ticket to privileges. Without the assignment notepad Webster does not earn evening privileges. The notepad is the ticket to television, stereo, phone, games, outdoors—in short, everything but breathing, eating, bathroom and of course, reading.

What if the notepad comes home without initials or without all necessary books? This is where the procedure most often unravels, and kids know it. They are incredibly resourceful at conjuring up explanations for a missing or incomplete notepad: "We had a substitute today, and he said he doesn't sign anything without having his lawyer read it first." "That kid, Butkus, made me eat the paper because he knew I'd get in trouble."

No matter what the reason, even if possibly legitimate, that notepad *must come home, signed and with books.* It is unquestionably your youngster's full responsibility. If you try to validate every excuse you hear, you're forcing yourself into a guessing game where facts are few.

If you don't want to curtail all the evening's privileges, you have another option, in some respects a better one. Beg, borrow or buy a copy of all your son's books to keep at home. If you can't get them, get something similar on his grade level from a local bookstore. Then, if *any* subjects are in question, you give assignments from your books and make sure your assignments are longer than anything he would have gotten at school. Your goal is to show him that it is definitely in his best interests to bring home all books and work.

Step 6. Persevere. The notepad procedure most likely won't work quickly. It may take weeks, months or even all year. For the first twenty-two days, Patience might play with her pencil and study the ceiling until 7:00 PM. Persist. A habit as longstanding as under-achievement doesn't pass quickly, no matter how consistent your methods.

To add effectiveness to the notepad procedure, keep several points in mind:

1. This approach is meant to be clear-cut and no nonsense. Your stance is nonnegotiable. Where your youngster's academic skills are concerned, you cannot afford to be irresolute. School is the work of children; it determines their future. In effect you are making a statement: at age fourteen you do not have free choice to do or not do your schoolwork.

2. The notepad will not immediately put schoolwork on Stanford's list of favorite things. It does not motivate him internally; it is pure external motivation. With time Stanford will develop some personal motivation because he'll see success,

and that will change his self-image as an underachiever. Until then you will be making him keep abreast of his work and learn the skills he'll need when he finally does decide to push himself.

3. Do not hover over, prod, threaten, debate or nag Stanford to complete his work. The problem is not yours; you have no reason to feel guilty. Help when you feel necessary, but otherwise let the approach do your talking. Stanford is fully aware of what the ground rules are. If he makes his life less pleasurable for a while, that is his choice. He is not foolish. He will motivate himself when he tires of his chosen life-style.

4. Set positive goals. For example, if Watson completes all classwork at school for three days in a row, he can earn a curfew extension. Gradually strengthen the requirements.

The notepad procedure is virtually foolproof if you stay with it. Once your youngster is convinced it's part of your house routine, he will work to make it unnecessary. In so doing he will no longer underachieve.

Double Jeopardy

Dear Dr. Ray,

I've always told my children, "If you get in trouble at school, you'll be in more trouble at home." My family tells me that I should let the school handle any problems there, rather than disciplining my kids a second time for an infraction.

Is Once Enough?

There's a legal concept called double jeopardy. It means you can't try someone again for the same crime if he's been acquitted the first time around. This makes for good law but not necessarily good parenting.

Sometimes two or more consequences may be warranted for one infraction. Further, what someone may consider innocent behavior you may not. A personal example may clarify some of this legalese.

Many years ago my son Andrew (now nineteen) threw some cornmeal at another boy in preschool. I'm pretty sure it was the other child's fault, but if not, it was probably somehow caused by my wife's parenting. The teacher assumed it was nothing malicious, separated him from the other child and sent a letter home to us about it.

Figuring that Andrew not only misbehaved but also cost me some business—I mean, who would want to bring their child to a shrink whose own kid acts up?—I asked him to explain.

"Well, Dad, I know some things are good to do, and some things are bad to do, but how can I know which is which until I try them all?"

A fast-on-his-feet answer, I thought. Nevertheless I told him he'd face some discipline at home for his behavior at school. My wife and I agreed: ten minutes in the corner, followed by a "forced nap" in bed. Also, no *Mr. Rogers* (it was the one where they showed how they put makeup on the Incredible Hulk, too!), no dessert after supper, no bedtime story, an early bedtime and a brief letter of apology to his teacher.

Andrew broke his teacher's rule, "No throwing." He broke our rule, "Respect your teacher's authority," the more serious rule.

Was this overdone? No doubt, many might think so, including Andrew's teacher. But my wife and I had this rationale: Andrew broke his teacher's rule, "No throwing." In addition he broke our rule, "Respect your teacher's authority," the more serious rule and thus deserving a more serious response.

Andrew's teacher's discipline—removing him from the scene of the cornmeal melee—was a beginning. The ending was left to us. We wanted to show Andrew that we would back his teacher not only in words but also in action. Our purpose was to send him a stronger message than his teacher could, given the constraints of her classroom. In essence our consequences had more meat than hers.

If you believe strongly that your children must respect their school—its teachers and its rules—you have a responsibility to hold them answerable to you, even if the school has addressed the trouble in their way. Don't let anyone tell you that you have no right to discipline according to your values and morals. If you are not being abusive or neglectful, you have a wide parental latitude in how you decide to deal with your youngster's misbehavior and growing pains. No one can take that from you in the name of psychological correctness.

Did Andrew ever throw cornmeal again? No, but we are working to help him overcome his phobia of grains.

Admit Your Limits

Dear Dr. Ray,

I recently discovered cigarettes in my fourteen-year-old son's coat pocket. I absolutely don't want him to smoke, but I'm not sure how to stop him.

Now What?

There's a saying that tries to capture the essence of raising kids: from birth to six you teach them; from six to twelve you guide them; from twelve to eighteen you pray for them. Certainly all teaching doesn't stop at age six; neither does guidance at age twelve. But most parents find that their rate of praying rises dramatically with the onslaught of adolescence.

Your concern over your son's smoking brings home one of the unalterable and scarier realities of parenthood: as a youngster's age increases, a parent's ability to supervise directly his behavior decreases. Ultimately that's good. From the day kids are born, we are aiming them toward their own independence and, for that matter, ours too. It seems poor timing, though, that our influence erodes faster than most of us are prepared for. Then again, we really never want to give up fully our parental status, no matter how old we get or how old they get.

You need to accept this truth: You can't stop your son from smoking—not totally anyway, for you simply can't shadow him every second of every day, nor would you want to. Letting him gradually pull away from your watchful eye is an indispensable part of his learning self-control and growing up.

Nevertheless, once you accept your declining influence, you may actually increase it. How's that again? Let me elaborate.

Your son is acutely aware that you can't monitor his every move. Kids realize this long before we parents do. So you're not giving away any parental secrets by informing him that you know he is smoking.

The forbidden fruit is not nearly so delightful when they know you know they're tasting it.

Convey to him your feelings about the issue—briefly. Don't carry on. I'm sure you've already walked over this subject many times in some way or another. Of course, I'm assuming you don't smoke. It's a bit hard to maintain credibility while you're lighting up one after another because you're so upset over his behavior.

Next tell him that you realize full well he can find plenty of places away from home to smoke, but you have no intention of trying to catch him. That would be a drag.

This "Admit Your Limits" approach is tailored for teens because it takes much of the fun out of misbehaving behind the folks' back. The forbidden fruit is not nearly so delightful when they know you know they're tasting it.

Your next step is to stand firm on those things you can control. To begin, there will be no smoking at home whatsoever. If any cigarettes or smoking paraphernalia are found, they will immediately be thrown out, with some type of consequence rendered. For instance, Carlton might lose his allowance for a period of time, since part of his money is being burnt up on cigarettes anyway. Or a fine of ten dollars can be levied and donated to the American Cancer Society. If his clothes smell of smoke, he washes them.

Further, should you find out that your son has been smoking—via a note from the school, report from a neighbor who saw him puffing down the street, the smell of his breath (he probably spends as much money on gum as on cigarettes)—consequences will be levied accordingly.

In essence, your whole message is, "I can't stop you from smoking. But you know how I feel. Be prepared to be held accountable if and when this behavior comes to my attention."

It's the nature of adolescence to behave sometimes in foolishly shortsighted ways. It's one way kids learn. It's a hard way, but they force themselves into it. If it's consolation, know that your son is likely to realize eventually the harm of cigarettes and thus develop some personal motivation to change his behavior.

SIX

Give Me Liberty, or Give Me New Parents

Teens want social freedom. They want lots more than is good for them. Parents must put limits on a teen's desires—often and firmly. And that's when the cycle begins.

You know better than they what is best for adolescents. They don't think you do. You try to convince them you do. They don't agree. You try harder. They get mad. Then you get mad. As the cycle repeats, it's tempting to compromise your better judgment because other parents have followed the path of least resistance or because the kids are relentless or simply for family peace.

Back to my first proposition: you *do* know what is best for your kids. Give social freedom slowly—much more slowly than all around you are giving it. You'll be glad you did. So too will your kids—eventually.

The Five *W*s

Dear Dr. Ray,

As kids head through their teen years, any ideas for better supervising their increasing social freedom?

Wary and Watchful

Begin by interviewing all their friends and their friends' parents. Determine which parents have the absolute best parental supervision and vigilance. Then double their standard for yourself and your kids.

My paramount rule for social supervision of teens (or any age): Never use the peer group of parents as your measuring stick. Most are giving too much freedom too early, too easily and too obviously. Too many are supervising with 20/80 foresight. Nowadays a parent needs 20/20 hindsight and 20/10 foresight.

A wise mother—in parenting, wisdom often comes through an accumulation of dumb decisions—told me that her kids never went anywhere without her knowing the five Ws: who, what, where, when and why.

> **In parenting, wisdom often comes through an accumulation of dumb decisions**

Who will you be with? This is possibly the most critical W. You don't need to be a shrink to know that who kids choose for company powerfully affects what they'll do when, where and how much. Can you pick their friends? No, but you'd better put nonnegotiable limits on whom they can pick. Parenting Law Number 101: know well—very well—their friends (and their parents), and you will safeguard very well your children's social well-being.

What will you be doing? This includes not only what is planned or what is happening the evening's first hour. Kids are notorious for starting at point A, as they dutifully told you, then (once out of sight) spontaneously adding points B, C and X to their itinerary. Changing plans is like changing planes. It needs to be cleared first with the control tower.

Inform Faith that you are a random caller. Anytime, anyplace, you could call just to say "Hi" and hear her voice. Call to a landline, not to a cell phone. Flouting teen protocol even further, you could ask to speak to a "who"—teen, adult or parent. Where your child's welfare is involved, embarrassment is not a mitigating factor.

Where are you going? Some *wheres* are simply off limits, even if the *who* is Biff, the school's PTA child of the year. If you aren't familiar with the *where*—often another teen's house—get familiar.

A note of caution: A five-minute call to a host parent in order to assess things is unreliable, especially if you're unfamiliar with the parent. Many is the mom or dad who was burned after concluding, "Freeman's mom said she'd be home the whole time," or, "The father seemed pretty strict," or, "They sounded like really nice people." Even shrinks don't assess someone's trustworthiness or maturity after a five-minute interview.

When will you be home? Of course, in many instances you will answer this one yourself. Let Dawn know that all *W*s are related. The *when* may routinely depend upon the *who, what* and *where*. Further, a broken *when* will render all other *W*s irrelevant for a while, as you will rethink all aspects of her social freedom.

Why are you going? This is often the least verifiable of the *W*s. Indeed, it may not always be that important. "Because I like being with my friends," or some variant thereof, might be acceptable to you given Walker's answers to the other *W*s. Then again, the activity itself may be OK but the motive bad. "I want to go swimming with Brooke"—a good *what* and a passable *who*. "Her boyfriend, Harley, and his biker friends are meeting us there"—a very bad *why*.

All five *W*s work in harmony. One unacceptable *W* can negate four acceptable ones. Also, all *W*s must be affirmed with the utmost trust-worthiness. Social freedom is founded upon character and judgment. It is not something that automatically accompanies age.

Former president Ronald Reagan's advice for dealing with foreign countries applies well to monitoring teens: trust but verify.

Old Young

Dear Dr. Ray,

My twelve-year-old thinks she's sixteen. She wants a lot more free-dom than I think is good for her age. How can I convince her she's not sixteen?

Aging Fast

You can't, not with words anyway. Once kids start creeping toward double-digit ages, they increasingly think they should be treated older than their age—in freedoms and rights, that is, not in duties and responsibilities. What twelve-year-old says, "Gee, Mom, I think I'm old enough to buy my own clothes and do my own laundry"?

The issue is not that your daughter wants more than you're willing to give her. Almost all kids want more than is good for them. And growing up is a push-and-pull negotiation with parents over how much we're going to give them when. The real issue is how to teach your daughter that, to the best of your ability, you will not allow her to grow up faster than her years.

Growing up is a push-and-pull negotiation with parents over how much we're going to give them when.

A good bit of your daughter's desire to be sixteen is driven by our society. Children are immersed in a popular culture that strips them young of their innocence. The world all around them relentlessly tempts them and tells them to be discontent with who they are and what they have. It offers them freedoms at ages when their counterparts of just a generation or two ago were still content to be kids. Consequently you are forced into vigilance, into resisting that culture for your daughter's sake, as you strive to give her a few more years of worry-free childhood.

I emphasize this to help you realize that what has always been natural to kids—pursuing more liberty than parents are willing to give— has been intensified dramatically by our society. You still can win, but it now takes far more effort to protect, supervise and say no.

So how do you keep a twelve-year-old a twelve-year-old, or a six-teen-year-old a sixteen-year-old for that matter? By treating her like a twelve-year-old or a sixteen-year-old or whatever she is. By giving and allowing her only what you judge is good for her, no matter what she thinks.

Your question, "How can I convince her she's not sixteen?" has two answers. You can't and you can. You can't in the sense that she seldom will agree with your stifling parental decisions. She's a child, and children are notorious for not seeing the world our way. But you can in the sense that you essentially will force your daughter to live as a twelve-year-old. With time she most likely will accept better her lot in life as a child with child freedoms, child privileges and child responsibilities.

Even the most stubborn reality resisters (a.k.a., children) eventually quit kicking and screaming against the wisdom of their parents. Some take months, some take years, and most become parents.

Doesn't it seem as if this is just one more example of life being wired backward? Children spend years wanting to be more grown-up than they are, only to one day be grown-up and nostalgically long for the simplicity and innocence of youth.

A Matter of Trust

Dear Dr. Ray,

Two times in two weeks my fourteen-year-old son was not where he told us he'd be with his friends. My husband says two weeks' grounding. I say indefinitely. What do you say?

Fooled Me Twice

I've been married twenty years. I have five daughters. I've learned to give the female perspective great consideration.

That said, I have a few questions. Where was your son when he was not where he should have been? It's one thing to stop at Burger Binge after the game without asking. It's quite another to head to Bambi's party, especially when Mr. and Mrs. Buck aren't home.

I'm going to assume, because of your reaction, that your son didn't just stop off at church to pray an extra half hour. He headed somewhere he wouldn't have a prayer of being allowed even if he had asked you on bended knee.

Next question: How do you know you were fooled twice? You may have been fooled more, but you were so fooled you never realized you were fooled. Discipline Reality Number 104: Teens usually do more things wrong than they're caught at. This isn't being cynical or untrusting of kids. This is accepting reality.

Almost everybody—young and old—does a lot more wrong than we're caught at. Since a primordial drive of adolescence is for more social freedom than parents know is good, it's only logical that periodically (or regularly) opportunity and temptation will overcome a youngster's conscience and fear of penalty.

I can't know, of course, where and how often your son has pushed his social boundaries, but you did catch him twice in only two weeks. You're either vigilant or lucky or both, or he's sloppy or guilt ridden or both. Either way, at the very least, in the future don't presume anything. Always have a way of checking.

Now, how long a grounding? Most parents are on the side of your husband. That is, if a youngster abuses a privilege, he loses the privilege for a set period of time, and then life returns to the pre-grounding state.

I, on the other hand, am on your side. And it's not just because you're a woman. Your son broke your trust—deliberately, it appears. You gave him freedom commensurate with your judgment of his trustworthiness. If he has shown you that you underestimated his judgment—when he is with peers, at least—then you need to reassess your judgment.

With both horses and teens, hold the rope close, letting it out by the inch as they settle.

One option is to curtail your son's freedom of movement for a while, as he reproves to you that he can be trusted. More closely monitor the *who, what, when* and *where* of his social world. Consider a two-week full grounding, followed by a clear holding in of the reins for as long as you judge necessary to teach the lesson and to restore your confidence in your son.

Raising teens is a lot like controlling a feisty colt. You have to hold the rope tightly and real close to his bridle. The more inches of rope between your hand and his head, the less you can direct him anywhere. With both horses and teens, hold the rope close, letting it out by the inch as they settle.

Some might disapprove of my comparing adolescent boys and horses. I understand. For one thing, training horses to cooperate is easier.

Trust Yourself First

Dear Dr. Ray,

How do we answer, "You just don't trust me," from our daughter? We supervise her socially far more than her friends' parents do their children. She's a good kid, but we still keep a close eye.

The Hawks

How short an answer do you want? How about, "I trust you. I don't trust the world." If you want something longer, I'll give it. I suspect, though, that your daughter probably won't accept it any better than my pithy sound bite.

You could say, "Oh, but I do trust you. I trust that you are fifteen. And I trust that fifteen-year-olds think like fifteen-year-olds. And I trust that there will be situations that, for all your wisdom, you'll be unsure how to handle. And I trust that with time, I'll allow you to experience more. And I trust that you'll believe me when I tell you I'm doing this out of love and to protect you, as a most precious gift from God."

Tell me, how could she not be moved by such an open expression of trust?

If after all this Faith still wants to call your vigilance a lack of trust, so be it. It's not that you don't respect her level of maturity. It's that you understand fully her youth. Don't allow Faith to make you feel

guilty by turning a positive—sound parental judgment—into a negative—a personal insult.

Why are kids so quick to take our loving supervision personally?
For one, humans in general are quick to take another's behavior personally. Call it the sensitivity of the self. For another, teens in particular are quick to misunderstand parents' motives. Therefore, to them
what you are doing stems from your inabil-
ity to see them accurately. You just don't
realize yet how trustworthy and downright
grown-up they are. In short, the problem,
dear parent, lies in your misperception, not
in their youth.

**Incomplete trust
isn't a bad thing,
socially or
psychologically.
It's recognizing
reality.**

Another reason kids freely fling the
"You just don't trust me" accusation is this:
it may be true; you don't fully trust them. And so? Incomplete trust
isn't a bad thing, socially or psychologically. It's recognizing reality.
Indeed, a wise parent realizes the limits of a child's judgment, experience and character. Even the most mature fifteen-year-old is still a
fifteen-year-old.

Other parents also fuel your daughter's fire. How? By letting their
kids do too much too soon. As Faith sees it, if all of those grown-ups
give more "trust" than you, you are the suspicious one. How could all
of them be wrong and you alone be right? If this were a game, the
score would be twenty-three (other parents) to two (you and your
spouse).

Here you face your toughest battle with your daughter. You know—
and I hope you act by your knowledge—that even if the score were
123 parents to you, it would be irrelevant. Good parenting is never
done by consensus. The question is not, how do my standards compare
to others? The question is, how do my standards reflect the kind of
child I wish to raise? If you believe Faith's friends have far too much
freedom for their age, then you must parent differently—sometimes

radically so, knowing that Faith won't always understand you. Someday she will, and that's what really matters.

For now the only foolproof way to convince your daughter that you do trust her is to give her all the freedom she wishes. But it's not worth going that far to be understood.

Under Contract

Dear Dr. Ray,

What do you think about using behavior contracts with kids?

Outbargained

It depends. Who will do your negotiating? Does your attorney specialize in behavior law? Is there a thirty-day notice of termination? An out clause?

Family therapists like behavior contracts. They are what the name implies: written agreements between parents and children laying out the terms and conditions of each party's responsibilities and earned privileges and the consequences for breaching the agreement.

Contracts, in my opinion, come with both assets and liabilities. Perhaps their main drawback is that all too often they are seen as a tool for compromise between equal partners.

Suppose that Dawn is appealing for an unlimited curfew. Parents counter with midnight. Well then, how about meeting somewhere near the middle, say 2:00 AM?

In the real world of parents and kids, parents should set most of the terms, as parents are—and should be—the governing authority.

In the real world of contracts, each party negotiates his best position. In the real world of parents and kids, parents should set most of the terms, as parents are—and should be—the governing authority.

If the parents' judgment is that midnight is best, then the only real bargaining points left might be 1) can Dawn earn extra privileges for honoring midnight? 2) what are the consequences for breaking curfew? 3) are there exceptions to the midnight rule?

Kids are naturally inclined to barter with parents, contract or no contract. The contract can convey the idea to Holmes that he now has an acceptable means to codify childish appeals. After all, Mom and Dad agreed to entertain his demands.

Beware also: Kids are superior negotiators. They don't need a lawyer. Their contractual skills are honed razor sharp from years of manipulating us, twisting our words and clouding the facts.

A third caveat: Set time limits on the agreement. Good parenting is flexible. Don't back yourself into terms that, depending upon the impulse of youth, would need to be rendered null and void. What if Dawn is caught severely abusing her social freedom? Might not the agreement of a midnight curfew have to be immediately terminated?

Contracts are not without benefits.

First, they can clearly enumerate your rules and terms. Less room is left for endless haggling every time a slightly different twist on a situation arises. Is midnight still in force on the Saturday you switch to Daylight Savings Time? What if Dawn is home at 11:59 but sits in the driveway until 12:37?

Second, a contract is as much for us as for our kids. Contracts legislate consistency. What we will do if Perry cooperates and what we will do if he doesn't is in writing. And anything that keeps us resolute and steady in our rules and discipline is good.

Third, contracts can help spouses present a more united front. The grown-ups have agreed publicly with each other to enforce expectations uniformly.

In the end contracts don't add much if parents have been clear and predictable in their rules all along. The kids have learned already that Mom and Dad mean what they say, whether it's written or not. In essence, where parenting is concerned, an oral contract is as binding as a written one.

Friends of a Feather

Dear Dr. Ray,

My sixteen-year-old is becoming friendly with a boy who has nearly total social freedom. I'm very uneasy with the association, but he says I can't pick his friends.

Picky

You're not picking his friends; you're putting limits on the pool of friends from which he can choose. "You can't pick my friends" is an absurd argument, but so many kids have flung it at so many parents—and so many "experts" have echoed it—that it can rattle parents. It can make them wonder if they really do have any right to protect a child from his poor social judgment.

To begin, you do a lot of picking for your son. You may not micro-manage each and every aspect of his life, but you put boundaries on almost all of it: what foods he can eat, what clothes he can wear, what money he has, what hours he can stay awake, what media he can hear and see and on and on. Indeed, it's your duty to select from what tries to come into your son's world.

Common sense, as well as social research, says that one's peers have power, at least as much power as clothes, money, media and all the other stuff parents moni-

Indeed, it's your duty to select from what tries to come into your son's world.

tor. Sadly, among teens, negative tends to influence positive more than the reverse. So, Mother, your instincts to protect are good. Don't second-guess them because of your son's psychological-sounding comeback.

Part of parents' reluctance to supervise friend choices comes from the idea that kids need to be social. True. That peer relations are part of growing up. True. That children eventually can sort through who is good to be with and who is not. False.

Humans are social beings. But in no way does that mean socializing in and of itself is always good for humans. It matters greatly with whom one is socializing.

A parallel can be drawn to literacy. Some argue that reading is so good for a child that what he reads is secondary, as long as he is reading something. No, bad reading can shape one badly. Bad friends can do the same.

If you believe this friend is potentially a very poor influence on your son, then you have every right to set boundaries, no matter what your son or some expert argues. Your boundaries may be absolute—no association with Freeman whatsoever—though at school this is tough to enforce. Or Freeman may come to your home, where he will be under your careful watch. Or you, your son and Freeman can be a social threesome to events. This will excite your son, I'm sure.

I don't think you'll really have to worry about the friendship lasting very long, even should you select the latter two options. If Freeman has as much social liberty as you say, he's not about to limit it by coming into your world or your son's.

Date and Age

Dear Dr. Ray,

My oldest daughter is fifteen. Most of her friends are beginning to date or have been dating for a while. In general, what do you think is a good age at which to allow children to date?

Aging Fast

When they're married. And only with their spouses.

Dating age depends upon all kinds of factors and varies from child to child, even within the same family. But here are some general guidelines from my experience.

1. Most kids are dating way too early.

2. Never consider the cultural "average age" when making your decision.

3. Start slow and supervised.

4. When in doubt, hold off.

5. Nothing is to be gained by premature opposite-sex involvement through dating or, for that matter, through phone calls, dances, parties or games.

This said, Life Truth Number 204 states that if you act differently than the majority does, you will be misunderstood by most. Let's suppose that you've decided to begin dating discussions when your daughter turns sixteen. Now, back in the old days—the early 1980s—you met resistance for such a decision mainly from the children. Parents used to instinctively expect to be challenged by their kids, especially in judgments of how fast one should grow up. What is quite different these days is that you are almost as likely to be questioned by your peers.

Life Truth Number 204 states that if you act differently than the majority does, you will be misunderstood by most.

"These are different times. This is not when you and I were growing up. These kids grow up so much faster nowadays. You can't protect them forever. You can't wrap a moral bubble around them; they have to deal with life."

"If you make kids too different, they'll feel like weirdoes who don't fit in. Then they'll get resentful and rebellious. I had a friend in California whose neighbor's boss had a son whose cousin's best friend wasn't allowed to date until he was seventeen, and I'll tell you, he turned his back on everything his parents had tried to teach him. When he got to college, he ran like a wild animal."

Yes, people have a penchant for arguing by exception. But a recent survey suggested that if a child has a first date between the ages of eleven and thirteen, he or she has an 80 percent probability of being sexually active during senior year in high school. First date at age fourteen leads to a 50 percent chance. First date at age sixteen, 20 percent chance. What chance would you prefer? What chance is much of society taking?

Key factors to consider in granting any type of dating freedom are the child's moral maturity, independence of thought, history of conduct in other social settings, strength of will, social judgment, choice of friends, responsibility toward schoolwork and respect for authority. I figure if I make the list long enough, my kids won't be eligible to date until they move out.

Once you are confident that your son or daughter has met these standards, sit them down, let them know how much you admire who they are and who they're becoming, then tell them, "Just three more years and you can date."

Just kidding. Sort of.

One Call From Your Cell

Dear Dr. Ray,

Almost all of my fifteen-year-old daughter's friends have cell phones. She's pushing hard, and her father sees nothing wrong with giving her one.

Just My Hang-Up?

Hello?!?

Want to hear a statistic, in my opinion a scary one? A recent survey said that 75 percent of kids between the ages of fourteen and seventeen have cell phones. The rest live in the Himalayas. Not really. The survey is of American teens.

Why am I scared by this? Because of early worries of brain damage caused by cell phones? Hardly. Because of talking while driving? Somewhat. Because of overblown bills? Sort of. My biggest fear? Cell phones open up to kids a whole new peer world that parents have a cell of a time monitoring.

Cell phones are wondrous pieces of technology. They have become nearly everyone's miniature companions. Even my eighty-year-old mother, long among inveterate cell-resisting adults, can't imagine leaving the house without her ever-present link to everybody.

The problem is not the technology itself, although it has changed dramatically our social landscape—some would argue for the better, some for the worse. Indeed, does anybody talk to anyone in person uninterrupted anymore?

Cell phones open up to kids a whole new peer world that parents have a cell of a time monitoring.

The problem comes when technology interacts with age, not my mother's, but with youth. Cell phones enable and encourage kids to reach out and touch someone, anyone, lots of anyones—some good to contact, some bad. It's really hard for a parent to know whom Belle is talking with about what, when and where and how much. Cell phones open up a much wider social world, a world that a parent can't oversee as well as she can a youngster's face-to-face interactions.

Most kids don't use a cell to break the law, buy marijuana or cheat on tests. The negatives of phone use are more subtle and insidious. They involve the most everyday communications between kids.

Teens have lots of immature ideas about what is socially cool, what is romantic, what is desirable, what is permitted, what can be gotten away with. Teens also can be pretty sheeplike. They are prone to the influence of the flock's ideas and behaviors. Cell phones are the perfect medium for teens to exchange all kinds of peer talk—some good, some bad, all private.

Part of growing up morally means not getting too enamored with popular peer group notions about life. This means parents have to keep a close ear on what things their kids are hearing, liking and considering.

"But, Dr. Ray, I want to know where my son is." Certainly. But how do you know for sure? Do you have the ability to trace the location of the call? Most cells don't come with GPS homing devices yet. A caller can call from anywhere. Locations are far easier to confirm with a landline.

"It's so much more convenient. They can call me when I need to pick them up." OK, purchase a phone with a ten-minute monthly limit. Or get one that only can receive or call out pre-programmed numbers. They have them now, even in the Himalayas. Or give the phone to Alexander only when he leaves the house for particular activities or reasons.

"It's for safety purposes." Refer to the above response. Look over each monthly call list. There should be no unexplained calls. If so, consider disconnecting for a time or indefinitely—your call.

I am not a back-to-nature psychologist. I am not recommending no cell technology whatsoever. I spend a lot more time on mine than I'd like. But I strongly advise that you resist the cultural flow on this decision. The fact that 75 percent of kids above fourteen have a cell does not make it good or socially healthy. Someday your daughter will have her own cell phone, and that day should not be when 92 percent of her friends have one but when you have judged her mature enough to use the cell phone wisely. Maybe when she's married.

One final call: ask your daughter, "Why do you want a cell phone so much?"

Savvy kids initially will cite the above reasons that most parents cite. They know what they're supposed to say. Give your daughter the responses I gave you. Then wait to see what other arguments she makes.

You might just hear some things that will confirm your impulse to hold the line. Get your husband to listen to this interchange. Call him on his cell if you have to.

Driving Ambition

Dear Dr. Ray,

The big D—driving—is coming up fast. My son has been riding me about it since he turned fifteen.

Nervous Wreck

Driving: to teens a standard entitlement; to parents an optional privilege. To teens a road to new freedoms; to parents a road to new worries. To teens a rite of adult passage; to parents fuel for nagging.

Teens live by the numbers. Indy thinks that because he has reached x years in life, certain rights must follow. Regarding driving, "I'm sixteen (or whatever the state's legal age is), so I should be permitted to operate a vehicle." To paraphrase Descartes, "I am, therefore I drive."

As I tell my own teens, "Sixteen is the minimum age at which the state tells me I can think about this. It is not the age it must happen." In other words, sixteen is really only another number, like four or eleven or thirteen and a half.

Nonetheless, because the state says it's now OK, or because most other parents agree with the state, or because teens are so hard-driving on this matter, most parents yield, even if their better judgment says, "Stop." Many's the mom or dad who would prefer to let Betsy mature a bit more before taking the wheel, but they compromise under the pressure.

As a parent of five children of driving age—nineteen, seventeen, sixteen, sixteen, fifteen and a half—and as a professional who's learned lots from years of riding shotgun with parents, let me offer some rules of the road:

The legal age is meaningless. What matters is the child's social and moral age. What is his level of trustworthiness? How cooperative is he at home? at school? with chores? How does he treat you? his siblings? Has he been responsible in things much smaller than driving? The best indication of how a youngster will guide a car is how he's guided his life up to this point.

The legal age is meaningless. What matters is the child's social and moral age.

Consistently I am stunned by parents who permit a license at the end of years of kid behavior that has been difficult, disrespectful and demanding. Their attitude seems to be, "Well, she is old enough, so I guess it's time." Or worse, "Life will be unlivable around here until I let her."

Never go against your better judgment because of pressure—be it from others, your schedule or your child. A privilege with as many features as driving needs lots of pondering, prudence and patience before it is allowed. Way too much is at stake for anything less. If in doubt, think longer, then delay.

You have the right to reassess your initial driving decision. Suppose you've judiciously weighed all the factors, and Van is now truly "old enough" to drive. (He is twenty-four.) What happens if he mishandles the privilege?

Most parents ground the child or remove the car. One option, but in matters of trustworthiness or integrity, a week or two without wheels may not be enough to teach the lesson. Time-limited grounding may have to yield to open-ended supervision. Only when you feel confident in Van's maturity does the door to driving open again.

On the day of license, along with the congratulations, inform Edsel that this is not his permanent license, as the state calls it. It is still a temporary permit, based upon his responsibility.

Implement a "good student" clause. Only sustained good grades lead to sustained license. Grades drop, license drops.

A clean car is a drivable car. That means your child keeps it that way, not you.

Gas and insurance cost money. Household cooperation is necessary to help pay operating costs.

Respect is a two-way street. Permission to drive is a parent's respect for the child's unfolding independence. A child's respect toward the parent is a must response.

Teens and most everyone else view driving as more age-related than character-related. Age is the least relevant factor in this decision. It all comes down to not what year the child was born but what year he has grown up.

Teens Are Like Airplanes

Dear Dr. Ray,

My teenagers are fourteen and sixteen. We disagree constantly over curfew times. Any suggestions for establishing reasonable limits? And how can I insure they'll be followed?

The Timekeeper

Let me begin with a safe assumption: Your idea of a fair curfew is earlier than your teens' and not the other way around. I did read once about a fifteen-year-old who argued for an earlier curfew than his parents had set. Last I heard, he was being studied at a leading university's Center for Unearthly Phenomena.

Actually parents and teens more often than not agree on what is a reasonable time to be home. We simply talk in different time zones. We parents can live with a

Parents and teens more often than not agree on what is a reasonable time to be home. We simply talk in different time zones.

midnight curfew and so can the kids, but we're talking midnight Eastern Standard Time and they're talking midnight Pacific Time.

Adolescents want later curfews because they believe, unlike their parents who have lived just a shade longer but who in the kids' eyes are no wiser for it, that they can handle responsibly the liberty of a later curfew. What parent hasn't met "Anything we can do at 1:00 in the morning we can do at 1:00 in the afternoon"? True. But we old-sters know that the potential for trouble and craziness rises steadily with each minute's journey into the wee morning hours. It isn't so much that we don't trust our kids; it's that we don't trust the others who are out and about at that hour.

Will kids understand your reasoning and willingly accept the curfew behind it? If they do, kiss them once for me. It's not standard "teenhood" to agree quietly to come home before one is ready. Teens like being out of the folks' eye- and earshot, especially at night. Something about the dark appeals to the independent streak in teens.

Regarding curfew guidelines, begin by seeking the kids' input about what they think is "fair"—that's a four-letter word that teens like to fling around a lot. If you can settle upon mutually agreeable times, you'll probably see more curfew adherence, as the kids have had some say in their limits. If, however, after sixty-two hours of nonstop nego-tiating through a federal mediator, you and Faith are still three hours apart, you must decide what is fair.

Some families set routine curfews—for example, 9:00 PM on week-days, midnight on weekends. Exceptions are made periodically based on such factors as special occasions, degree of supervision or Gardiner's promise to mow the lawn for the next seven years without being asked. Maybe Barbie is double-dating with her boyfriend's par-ents to the ballet (right!); curfew here might be extended to 1:30 AM.

On the other hand, Oliver wants to use your two-day-old van to take his girlfriend to a quadruple feature at a drive-in somewhere across thestate line. In this instance you might move curfew to 8:00 PM, an hour before the first movie starts.

Some parents have no set curfews, instead judging each request on its merits or lack thereof. This can work, but it carries more risks for arguments, and each evening out can become a rowdy negotiating session.

Whatever approach you take, the curfews you establish depend upon you, your household, your youngsters and your situation. Resist the temptation to allow a curfew you feel is unwise because "there's not even enough time to get anything to eat after the game," or "not a single guy in the whole school will ask me out because I have to be in so early," or "you just don't trust me," or "come on, Dad, these are different times from when you were growing up." Regarding this last one, indeed they are. All the more reason for curfews.

Kids will present all manner of curfew commentary. Most of the time this is a sign that you are disagreed with—not unloved, not disrespected, not necessarily even thought unfair, just plain disagreed with. And hasn't that happened many times before on issues much smaller than curfew?

There's a bright side to working out a curfew. Even though it can cause agitation, it'll help you sleep better. An adolescent's curfew time, followed closely by the sound of a key in the door, almost always translates to a lying-in-bed-wide-awake parent finally beginning to nod off.

Now, onto the acid question: How can you insure that Faith will live within her curfew? Acid answer: You can't. The ultimate reality of any discipline is that you never can guarantee that your youngster will exercise good judgment. Only she can guarantee that. You can do much, however, to make it more likely that she will act responsibly.

Obviously, it would be untrusting, not to mention inconvenient, for you to shadow Faith everywhere and escort her home at the appointed hour. You would stand out conspicuously at any teen gathering. Your jeans aren't faded enough, and they don't have anywhere near enough holes. What's worse, you still believe dance partners should be at least in the same room.

No, with any curfew, you're implicitly making a statement of trust: I believe you'll be home when I've asked you to. Should Faith not be home at a "decent hour" (I'm sure she sees nothing decent about it), then she needs to know there are consequences for tardiness. Here are ideas.

1. Football games, dates, sensitivity encounter groups and so on are privileges, and a privilege abused is a privilege lost, at least temporarily. A basic house curfew rule might be that each fifteen minutes late leads to one day of grounding. The days would best be predetermined, preferably Friday or Saturday. If you leave the choice up to Dawn, she'll choose to stay home on Monday afternoon and Wednesday evenings.

2. Old-fashioned grounding still works well—although it's always amazed me how often we feel we can't live in the same house with that kid for one more minute, and then we turn around and force her to stay home.

3. A more specific curfew rule is that for every one minute late without a solid, verifiable reason, five minutes will be taken off the time a youngster has to be home on the next occasion out. You could use any ratio you wish: five minutes late costs fifteen; fifteen costs an hour; ten costs ten.

4. Using the one-for-five example, let's say that Knight drifts in at 12:36 AM with the excuse that the electricity in the gym went out for thirty-six minutes (excuse rating: fairly original, too verifiable, overall nice try). So, 36 x 5 = 180 minutes = three hours earlier Knight has to be in the next time he wants to go somewhere. If normal curfew tomorrow night is midnight, he has to be in by 9:00. Brace yourself, you're likely to hear something like "It's not even worth going out if I have to be in by 9:00." Probably not.

5. Curfew consequences cut both ways. If Faith follows her

curfew, conducting herself responsibly while she's out, then periodically it might be wise to relax the limit by one hour or so. Your message is, "Responsibility begets freedom."

Whatever curfew consequences you choose, the common denominator is that they are not threats to be flung at retreating backs as Robin flies out the door. They are pre-established, automatic house rules designed to improve parental supervision and keep peace.

In the end, no matter how responsible your youngster is, periodically you probably will have to enforce your rule, because teens are like airplanes. Their scheduled arrival time doesn't always coincide with their actual arrival time.

The Online Bottom Line

Dear Dr. Ray,

If I let them, my kids would live on the computer. I don't think it's a good place to live.

Virtually Ignored

Every computer must have a monitor—a really, really good one. Otherwise the computer is useless. What kind of monitor do I recommend? A parent—a really, really good one. Otherwise the computer is more than useless; it is treacherous.

I am stunned at how many parents permit kids to head into computer land with no more limits than the child's own self-control. A recent survey said that only 17 percent of parents monitor their kids' computer use.

Computer technology is mind-numbing. It allows a child to talk to anyone else in the world, visit any place in the world and see anything in the world—good or bad, helpful or hurtful, friend or fiend. Simply put, something so technologically powerful needs powerful safeguards. Anything less is like putting a machine gun in the hands of a three-year-old. The potential for damage is enormous, and it's only a matter of time.

I'm no computer geek. Only last week did I figure out how to Windex the screen. But I am a child-rearing geek. So I have some basic commands to make you a better monitor.

1. Get the absolute best filter you can find. Get a professional to help you, if necessary. No filter is foolproof, but screen out as much unwanted, sleazy, awful stuff as is humanly possible. I know many parents who didn't, and are they regretful now.

2. Consider having a password to log on. This will keep the computer off limits if you are not home or do not want the computer on. You can specify that any misuse or abuse of the computer will lead to a period of password-only access.

3. Even *if* the password's in place, even *if* the filter is superb, even *if* you know exactly what Gates is doing online, limit his time. The computer may have even more socially stunting and addictive potential than television. People, especially kids, need to interact with real people in real situations, in real time and real lots. How many husbands nowadays spend far more time with their screen than with their real-life spouse? If you let it, the computer will be a tireless piece of technology usurping your children's time and attention. And it is so good at it.

4. Keep the computer(s) in a well-traveled, observable family place: the kitchen, dining room, family room. Two of the absolute worst places are the basement and a child's room. A TV in a kid's bedroom is foolish; so too is a computer.

5. Dramatically limit, if not prohibit, communication in chat rooms, personal blogs and instant messaging. You can't-know—and neither can they—with whom they're interacting. And even if you and they do know, you really can't monitor what is said about what and whom and how it is said.

In our home the older teens can only instant message friends in supervised, school-related forums. Even then, if we read anything at all objectionable, that avenue is closed for a specific amount of time—a long time.

Just because a technology is available doesn't mean one has to use it, particularly if the user's judgment and maturity are still forming. Too many parents come to understand the computer's dangers only after their child has experienced them personally.

What about doing homework on the computer? Refer here to commands 1 through 4. Then be extra-vigilant. Oxford knows you think he's working diligently, so you're less likely to observe closely what he's doing. Check, and do so regularly. It's not that I think teens are sneaky or slick—well, OK, some—I just recognize the power of relentless temptation. If they can't resist it, we have to help.

Anything less is like putting a machine gun in the hands of a three-year-old. The potential for damage is enormous, and it's only a matter of time.

Are all of my stern warnings simply roundabout ways of crying, "Trash the computer"? No, not at all. For better or worse, more parts of our lives are becoming computer-linked every day. But given the virtually unlimited communication and visual power of the computer, we need to keep it under severe control. Otherwise it won't be our servant; it will be our master.

SEVEN

Standing Strong

A safe observation: Good parents have higher standards than their teens do. This is not brilliant insight; it has been so throughout time. That's why kids need parents: to teach them a better way.

Only in the last generation or so have good parents faced resistance from a most unexpected source: other parents. Those supposed to see parenting through grown-up eyes are instead compromising and lowering their standards closer to their teens' level. Consequently the best of parents now need to stand stronger, not just with the juveniles but also with other adults.

Great parenting is not majority parenting. Hold fast to your high standards, supervision and discipline, no matter how others are holding to theirs! Time, and your children, will prove you right.

Do Mistakes Make Maladjustment?

Dear Dr. Ray,

I guess I read too much. I'm always worried that I'm going to do something wrong as a parent, something that will cause emotional problems now or later in life.

Tentative

Your question underscores what may be the most haunting fear among good parents today: the fear of making a child-rearing "mistake" that will lay the groundwork for psychological damage. What's more tormenting is that you can't know when or where the damage is going to surface because it's buried deep within a youngster's psyche, festering for years until rearing its ugly head. And when it does, you have to wonder helplessly what you "did wrong."

Seventeen years from now, is your daughter going to be sitting in the middle of some encounter group, along with seven other ex-embezzling parolees—she's their leader—talking about you and the turning point in her life?

"I've never shared this with anyone before. I was barely five years old. My mother was screaming my full name over and over from the garage, along with words I couldn't understand. When I answered she said, 'Go to your room and don't come out until you're married.' Then she threw my Care Bear under the truck tires and started driving back and forth over it, laughing hideously and promising that she'd never buy me anything ever again if I couldn't keep it where people wouldn't trip over it.

"I was never the same after that. When I was six I started counter-feiting school lunch tokens. A year later I wrote my first bad check."

How can you possibly parent, much less enjoy it, under such a black cloud, under the constant fear that if you miscalculate, misjudge, lose your cool or make any other human miscue, you run the risk of setting in motion a chain of emotional events that will culminate in a social misfit?

Charity hates to share with her brother. If you make her do so, will she grow up hating all men? The only way to get Newton to do his math homework is to require that he finish it immediately after school before he goes outside to play. He hates this rule and fights it. Is he eventually going to be so turned off toward numbers that he'll become a fifteen-year-old sixth-grade dropout? Day-to-day parenthood requires so many decisions and judgments that you could keep yourself in perpetual turmoil second-guessing every move you make.

The experts have done a lot to scare parents. Recently a colleague saw a "family specialist" on national television tell parents that the absolute worst thing they could do to their children—it would lead to all manner of addictions and psychological imbalance—was to be inconsistent. What parent isn't?

In fact, what is the defining characteristic of human beings? Inconsistency. There is not one of us who is consistent in parenting or anything else. We may strive toward it, but we'll never get there. And now we've been told that because we are what we are, we'll ruin our kids! One parent shared, "Reading all this stuff makes me feel as if the worst thing for a child is a parent."

Parents must allow themselves to be human. Good parenting is a process of learning from good and bad moves alike. You'll make plenty of poor decisions. You'll say things you shouldn't. You'll overreact, denying John bathroom privileges for three months because he left his underwear on the towel rack again. (Of course he'll use the standard defense, "Dad

"Reading all this stuff makes me feel as if the worst thing for a child is a parent."

leaves his underwear there too." Then from the far corner of the garage, you'll both hear, "When you start paying the bills around here, young man, you can leave your underwear anywhere you want!")

Two other realities make it likely that, in sum total, you will make more mistakes than your parents did, even if you're a better parent. The first is that childhoods are getting shorter. Nine-year-olds now face what twelve-year-olds a generation ago—what fifteen-year-olds two generations ago—used to face. The world is fast becoming a tricky, seductive place. If it's harder for a child to grow up, it will be harder for a parent to grow up too, and more mistakes will be made along the way.

The second reality is that while childhoods are getting shorter, parenthoods are getting longer. In past generations, after eighteen years or so, the kids left to try life on their own. Nowadays, twenty-six or twenty-seven years after birth, they're still hanging around. They might leave for a couple of years, just to tease you, but soon they're back, with their friends and the bus and their laundry, shouting at three in the morning, "Guys, we can stay a little while, a couple of years anyway. Mom will put food on the table between washing the white and color loads. She likes to cook big breakfasts and do laundry."

Parenthood is not for the faint of heart. It's as demanding as it is rewarding. In the end the whole picture is what counts. And for most of us, the good moves far outnumber the bad.

Pick Your Battles?

Dear Dr. Ray,

People often advise me, "Pick your battles," with my children, but I'm not sure exactly what that means or how to do it.

Battle Fatigued

"Pick your battles" has become a parenting mantra among the experts, a sort of cliché, capable of being shaped into all sorts of meanings. Whether it's good for your child rearing or not depends upon how you apply it.

At one level I wholeheartedly agree with picking your battles. Much of what any child does that irks a parent is not wrong. It is not immoral, hurtful, defiant, dangerous or irresponsible. It is kid junk, the stuff of childishness.

A personal scenario: Sometimes, while riding in our van, several of our children, usually the younger and more tone deaf, decide to sing. In itself I suppose this would be tolerable, but they all sing different songs, with made-up words, in poor timing and with gusto. While grating to our ears, I don't think they're doing anything wrong, at least for the first thirty-six seconds or so. They're just being kids, however bizarre. But if either my wife or I asks them to tone it down or to stop so we can converse without screaming, they'd better, not only for our sanity but to show respect. We, as parents, have a right to put a ceiling on the chaos, little battle or not.

There is one meaning of "pick your battles" that drastically undercuts good parents' efforts to raise great kids. It is this: Stand firm on the major moral stuff, but be flexible on the minor moral stuff, especially if your youngster is overall a "pretty good kid."

Suppose your thirteen-year-old son, Sting, wants to attend a rock concert with his buddy Ringo. By today's standards the concert is relatively benign. The group, "Kids in Charge," has had only two minor felonies and a pending drug probe. But you're against it. Sting's too young; there is no adult supervision; the scene is just too crazy.

Now, some experts (probably those without thirteen-year-olds) would advise: Find a compromise. Don't strive for unconditional victory, because Sting could resent you or fight back harder. Let him go if he takes a cell phone and checks in with you. Maybe Ringo's dad will go with the boys. Or if the rock concert is out, how about a free trip to three movies of his choice instead? After all, you don't want to be rigid.

Where your child's morals are at stake, if someone advises you to pick your battles, ignore that advice.

This expert's advice? Maybe here you do want to be rigid. Your child's character and moral protection are involved; therefore, the battle is important. Where your child's morals are at stake, if someone advises you to pick your battles, ignore that advice.

A more common conflict: suppose Rocky constantly torments his sister Adrian. Since sibling squabbling is "normal," shouldn't you overlook most of it? How about no punching in the face and no name-calling? Run-of-the-mill torments—that is, words, looks or put-downs—are small arms fire and can be ignored.

Wait a minute! Is it wrong or isn't it to mistreat someone? If you think it is, then sibling respect is a battle to pick and to win, no matter how "small" the wrong.

One last salvo: When you pick your battle, don't battle. Stand confident and strong. Enforce your decisions with love and discipline, not arguing, endless lectures and nagging. The more quickly the "battle" is over, the better for all, and the fewer battles you will confront in the future, as your child learns clearly where the moral line is drawn.

Rebelling Without a Cause

Dear Dr. Ray,

What do you think about the idea that if parents are "too strict" or put their moral standards too high, ultimately a child will rebel?

Strict but Wavering

Of all the parent-assaulting, authority-undercutting ideas that blanket the child-rearing landscape today, this one gets my vote for ranking among the worst. How's that for psychologically sugar-coating my answer?

Certainly, if a parent is dictatorial and unloving, he or she risks raising a child who sees little rationale or warmth underlying the standards and who may ignore or challenge those standards with time. As the saying goes, "Rules without relationship can breed rebellion."

The critical difference between strong parenting with love and strong parenting without love, however, is often ignored. Implicitly the warning is that no matter how much you love your child, if you expect too much good behavior or you are too different from the parenting crowd, you're asking for psychological trouble. Your high expectations will be the very thing leading to your child's unruliness. This notion finds face in the stereotype of the "preacher's kid," who as everyone knows is the sneakiest, most morally profligate kid of the bunch.

Truth be told, most preacher's kids are more moral and mature than the norm. False notions are fueled by the exceptions that do fit the stereotype.

Some kids will rebel against good rules and limits regardless of how loving their parents are. As long as free will exists, there are no parenting guarantees. But again these are the exceptions, and of these, many only temporarily rebel before finally and fully embracing what they were taught for years.

The most crippling aspect of this nutty notion is that it keeps parents from resolutely taking the stands that deep down they know are right. After all, Dorothy already thinks she has the Wicked Witch of the West for a mother and Attila the Hun for a father. So you'll only make things worse by being "too controlling" in your rules. You need to compromise your moral position here and there so as not to appear unreasonable.

Once upon a time, back before the onslaught of all the experts and their theories, parents instinctively understood that it was healthy to set high standards and enforce them vigorously. Now this instinct is being challenged. Set your bar too high, the new wisdom says, and your children's resistance is a sure sign that you're being too pushy about this whole parenting thing. On the contrary, it's a sure sign that you're a parent and your kid's a kid.

Once upon a time, parents instinctively understood that it was healthy to set high standards and enforce them vigorously.

But what if you are clearly way above the parenting norm in your social supervision, in the chores you require, in the respect you expect and so on? Won't your kids draw comparisons? Sure, they will. They'll resist you more than they would if more people thought as you do.

Keep your standards high. The results you want—great kids—will happen, even if your ride is bumpy and you are misunderstood along the way.

One more thing: Just because you set your moral sights high for you and your children doesn't mean you'll get there consistently. That's kids. Indeed, that's us. Be prepared always to teach and discipline, and over time your high standards will become the norm for your family. And other parents will begin to wonder how you are raising such good kids who aren't as rebellious as theirs.

Face the World, Kid!

Dear Dr. Ray,

I try hard to keep my kids innocent and to raise them more slowly than their peers. Regularly I hear, "You can't protect them forever. That's a real world out there. They have to learn to deal with life."

Cautious Mom

Yes, you can't protect them forever. Yes, that is a real world out there. And yes, they do have to learn to deal with life. What does any of this have to do with raising your children at your pace and not the world's?

What you are hearing makes my top ten list of nonsense notions assaulting good parents today. Mindlessly repeated by so many so often, these notions have assumed the illusion of child-rearing truth. They are "correct" just because everybody is saying they are.

Let's go back a couple of generations when it was considered intrusive and impolite for people to give you their unasked-for opinions about your parenting. Protecting kids—socially, morally and emotionally—was considered a very good thing. Indeed, a prime duty of grown-ups was to shield children from the ugly and immoral stuff of life while morality was being formed. Keeping kids innocent was a worthy goal, a sign of responsible and wise parenting. Soon enough a youngster would face what was out there beyond childhood.

In the last generation or two, we've taken a step backward toward "enlightenment." It is now more psychologically savvy to help kids deal with seamy reality as it assails them. In fact, if you put this off too long, when the child finally does confront the "real world," whatever that means, he will be shell-shocked emotionally and morally. He'll be overwhelmed or seduced by evil or crushed into despair. His very innocence will be his undoing.

I have some questions regarding this "real kids know the real world" assertion. Who is better able to navigate the temptations and challenges of life, a mature child or an immature child? Who is more able to cope with life's ugliness, a moral eight-year-old or a moral eighteen-year-old?

The opposite of innocence is not maturity; it is worldliness. And worldliness doesn't equip a child to cope with the world. It just makes him more likely to be comfortable with it.

Most parents accused of being overprotective are not "babying" their children emotionally, nor are they running ahead of their kids, bulldozing all of life's obstacles and frustrations out of the way. Their protectiveness is morally driven. They want to shield their kids from situations and people who could overwhelm their judgment or their young consciences. A good parent's supervision, caution and vigilance are healthy and wise.

The opposite of innocence is not maturity; it is worldliness.

Only when it's too late do many parents realize that they weren't protective enough. Over and over again my experience with families has taught me a real life truth: far more children have trouble as adults not because they grew up slowly but because they saw and learned too much too early.

So stand strong, Mom. Give social freedom later than the peer group gets it. Protect innocence. Lay a strong moral base before you let the world assault it. Your "overprotectiveness" will be rewarded by real life.

He's Just a Kid

Dear Dr. Ray,

Is it my imagination, or are more and more parents getting criticized by others for disciplining their kids?

Getting Criticized

If it's your imagination, then you and I share the same fantasy life.

A mother once called my radio show with the following scenario. She and her two daughters (ages twelve and fourteen) were attending a pool party. Come dusk, the hostess asked the parents to shepherd the kids out of the pool. Several parents took up negotiating positions poolside and began to ask, nag, bargain and promise red Corvettes to their kids in reward for cooperation.

Mom said she walked to the pool, caught her daughters' attention and wordlessly motioned with her hand for both to exit the water, whereupon the girls climbed out, dried off and sat down. The other parents observed the contrast between these girls' cooperation and their kids'. Mom told me, "We became the talk of the party after that."

What do you think the other parents talked about? If you surmised something like, "How did she do that?" you would be as wrong as I was. The general feedback Mom heard was, "It's not normal for kids that age to be so cooperative. We wonder what goes on at home for them to be so afraid of you."

Something that was once a valued, admired result of strong discipline—a child's cooperation—was being interpreted as a bad thing, as some kind of psychological intimidation. The girls weren't learning to obey their mother's God-ordained authority; no, they had become Stepford kids, walking in robotic lockstep to the she-tyrant's dictates.

How did some adults get so warped in their view of healthy discipline? The many answers to that question would take us far beyond the bounds of our space here. Let's cite briefly only a few.

The experts. As a group they have preached for decades that the modern enlightened means to elicit kid cooperation is through words and reason. If that fails, discipline is a last resort, but it should still be employed in a benign way. This mindset has permeated "proper" child raising. Thus, those who are strong parents are seen as psychological throwbacks, parenting barbarians who don't realize what they are doing to their kids' psyches.

The culture. We are far less respectful of authority in our society than we were a few generations ago. Many people view authority from anywhere—parents, teachers, police, military, employers, the Church—as an instrument for stifling personal autonomy and expression. The legitimacy of authority is always open to question, particularly when it tells people to do something they don't want to do.

Child development theories. Merely because of age, adolescents as a group are supposed to be uncooperative, moody and obnoxious. So says modern child-rearing theory. Therefore, any kid who becomes more likeable as she approaches fourteen, or still respects her folks, or enjoys being with them or matures smoothly could be considered a bit of an aberration, not quite "teen normal," if you will.

> **The legitimacy of authority is always open to question, particularly when it tells people to do something they don't want to do.**

For one real-life example that shatters this developmental myth, you need only look to home-schooled kids. Because they are far less soaked in the peer group's mentality and ways, they don't seem to become quite so pop-defined as "teenagers."

So it's not at all in your head. Good discipline isn't as universally admired as it once was. Be confident that you're on the right track, even though others question you. Your children will provide indisputable evidence that your way was the right way.

An Army of One

Dear Dr. Ray,

My kids (boy, thirteen, girl, fifteen) regularly inform me of how much more their friends are allowed to do. And the sad fact is, the kids aren't lying. Their friends are allowed to do more—lots more.

Close to Alone

Back in the Mesozoic Era—the mid-1970s—when we threw other parents at our parents, they knew it was mostly bluff. Fact was, many if not most parents thought and did somewhat alike. So when we negotiated with Mom by citing Dawn's mom, who trusted Dawn to set her own curfew, she was pretty secure in replying, "Well, Dawn's mom isn't your mom; I am." Or, "When you live at Lucky's house, you can do what he does." Or my dad's classic, "If Marlin jumps in the lake, are you going to jump in too?"

Nowadays, as more parents get laxer, the stronger parents are feeling isolated. Further, as you've noticed, this "guilt by comparison" tactic is no longer mostly ploy; it's fast becoming reality. Any kid, without conducting even one tracking poll, can cite ten or twelve families whose standards and supervision are more kid-friendly than yours. And since kids judge quality by the numbers, you are supposed to feel pretty Neanderthal about that. Indeed, the standard rationale underlying all comparing is, "How can all those parents be wrong and you be right?"

To which savvy parents should reply, "They are, and I am."

To avoid being bullied by the "You're not mainstream" accusation, hold fast to several truths:

1. There are parents out there who think as you do. They may not be visible to you, as some may be keeping a low profile for fear of being targeted as "too strict" or "too controlling." Then too, your teens, even if aware of such cultural cave dwellers, are not about to suggest them as good role models. When was the last time you were hit with, "But, Mom, Gabby has no cell phone, is only allowed three hours of TV per week and does chores until noon every Saturday. Her parents are just too cool"?

2. Consensus parenting is not wise parenting. The majority often doesn't provide a good example. If your way isn't aligned with the group's, it may be that your way is better. By statistical definition, the higher up you go, the less like others you are.

3. Numbers can indicate preference and not "rightness." If 83 percent of thirteen-year-olds receive more than your son's five dollars per week allowance, or if 96 percent of fifteen-year-olds have their own rooms, so? (as my sister used to say to me). Your parental judgments are based upon your life, your morals, your family and your kids. You're not wrong because most choose differently. You may be perfectly right being one in a hundred, given your unique situation. Sometimes just being your youngsters' parent makes you right.

4. Your kids may be trying to cast you as a lone parenting wolf, but that doesn't mean they're completely running with the pack. Somewhere in their little psyches may lurk, despite all the bluster and recriminations, a little bit of gratitude for your tough but caring stance. For the moment their upset is their ruling emotion, but don't discount a delayed reaction born of security and respect. How delayed? Till they have teenagers? Actually it could be happening even as they speak, though they'd never admit it.

An axiom of statistics is, the real good and the real bad are real uncommon; they're far out of the normal range. Apply that to parenting. The better you strive to be, the less "normal" you are.

One more reassurance: Your home is not merely a place of strict rules, unyielding limits and arbitrary dictates—at least I hope not. Your high standards are within the embrace of love, warmth and togetherness. These soften and eventually will eliminate any lingering teen resentment over your extreme way of raising children.

An axiom of statistics is, the real good and the real bad are real uncommon.

Your kids may judge your parenting by what they feel now. But the true judge of your parenting is what they think ten years from now.

Something tells me they'll be pretty grateful for their army of one mom.

Mom's the Boss

Dear Dr. Ray,

My dad was a strong authority during my childhood. In my family I'm the strong authority. How common is this?

Mom

One thing's for sure: It's more common than it used to be. More and more moms are telling me—usually in exasperation—that they are the disciplinarians in their homes. They set the limits, the structure and the rules.

The refrain sounds something like, "I know my discipline style isn't the greatest. I tend to talk too much, negotiate and nag, but at least I'm trying—unlike Disney Dad over there or Mr. Oblivious or Mr. Laissez-faire or Mr. 'Honey, I was that way when I was a kid, and I turned out OK.'" (Some ladies may have to resist the riposte, "Can we vote on that?")

Yes, your situation seems, if not all too common, not all that unusual. During parenting presentations, when I speak about this phenomenon, invariably I see women's elbows meet men's ribs, knowing glances from mate to mate, sheepish husbandly smiles and "This shrink has you pegged" wifely looks.

Let me speak briefly to the men, then to the women.

Guys, next time you hear your wife locked in a verbal battle with a child, don't sit barco-lounging in the other room thinking, "If I close my eyes, I can't tell which one of them is the twelve-year-old." Get up, enter the scene and pull the plug. "That's not just your mom you're talking to that way. That's my wife. Go to your room. I'm going to ask your mom and my wife what she wants me to do about this. And then I'm going to do more."

Gentlemen, you do this a few times, and you'll see warmth from the ladies for hours. Sometimes I give my boys a couple of bucks and tell them, "Go give your mother grief. I'll be right in." Just teasing. I don't really have to pay them to give her grief.

This approach won't balance out the overall exercise of parental authority. But it is a natural place to begin. And it makes women feel very valuable.

Ladies, however frustrating it is to be the lead disciplinarian most of the time, remember that you also have most of the leverage. Let's say you impose on Charity a five-hundred-word essay for her surly lack of gratitude, along with a two-day grounding. What if Dad isn't with you but is being passively unsupportive or actively undercutting? Either way you have quiet power. Who does most of the taxiing? Who plans and cooks meals? Who washes the clothes? In most families, even if Mom works outside the home, she still does the majority of daily childcare. And that gives her the majority of discipline clout.

When you have leverage, you don't need to talk so much, negotiate and nag.

If Dad doesn't support the grounding, is he willing to take Charity to practice? Will he wash her uniform? Will he pack her lunch? Will he take her to baby-sit?

Certainly I'm not advocating you cause marital strife. I only am pointing out that when Mom sets most of the expectations and rules, automatically she maintains control of most of the discipline leverage. And when you have leverage, you don't need to talk so much, negotiate and nag. In time, hopefully your husband will see a calmer, more resolute mom who doesn't get emotionally carried away but in fact uses real authority to get cooperation.

Oh, yeah, men, one final point, and don't take this as nagging. Your wife's style may sometimes be too wordy or too moody, but that does not reduce her God-given authority. Don't minimize her motherly role because she doesn't always exert it well. Besides, if she gets more support from you, she may feel and act less frustrated.

Then you will be better able to tell which one is the twelve-year-old.

Attitude of Gratitude

Dear Dr. Ray,

My fifteen-year-old daughter embarrassed herself and me at her birthday party. She acted very ungrateful for her gifts. How can I teach her to be more appreciative of all she has?

Grateful for an Answer

Give her less. That's my short answer, but I'll give you more. Happy birthday.

There's a direct relationship between what kids have and how grateful they are for it. Put simply, the more they get, the less they appreciate it. Because of the complexities of human temperament, this is not a perfect relationship, but it's about as close as any you'll find in parenting.

Since the setting for your daughter's ingratitude was a birthday party, let's stay there for a while. During birthdays a child is not only center stage—as she should be, because it's her party—but she is also the focal point of divergent streams of gifts. If your daughter's birthday is like most these days, the gifts number somewhere between ten and twenty, and that's not counting the gifts given to siblings so they don't feel "left out." (For the life of me, I don't know how that practice got started. Siblings *should* feel left out of the gifts; it's not their birthday.)

If in your judgment all is too much, store some for later, give some away and pitch anything objectionable.

Because your daughter is given too much materially—at birthdays or otherwise—doesn't mean you have to stand by passively and let her have it all. If in your judgment all is too much, store some for later, give some away and pitch anything objectionable. Through learning that life is not a candy store with limitless dispensers, your daughter will learn that receiving is a privilege, not a right.

One mother told me, "My son has really come a long way in showing gratitude. At his birthday party he received a toy he already had, and he didn't throw it." That's progress, I guess, but my unspoken question was, "And what did you do about those times when he did throw it?" My wife, to whom I later told this story, answered the question her way: "He would have lost not only his unwanted duplicate but probably every other toy he received that birthday."

Children don't feel appreciation or gratitude naturally. They learn it by slowly coming to understand that much of what they receive is not an entitlement. And when they act as if it is, we must act to show them it is not. How? By giving them less than they want and by expecting them to act with gracious appreciation when they receive. If they don't, they will lose what they thought was theirs.

In so much of human maturity, the act precedes the feeling. If we parents don't require grateful behavior, it is unlikely that an attitude of gratitude will ever develop.

Grated by Ingratitude

Dear Dr. Ray,

I'm getting really tired of my fourteen-year-old daughter's complaining attitude. It's particularly frustrating because she doesn't seem to realize how good she has it.

Grateful for Ideas

Are you complaining? A core rule of life—as it is rooted in human nature—is that people become less grateful the longer they have it better. What starts out as gratitude for good things becomes expectation for good things, which becomes demand for good things. Quite bluntly, it is tough for people, young or old, not to complain more as life improves.

Most parents believe we had it tougher as kids than do our kids. "When I was a boy, I used to walk eighteen miles to school, uphill both ways, in a foot of nuclear waste. My turn to wear the one pair of shoes only came around every two weeks, and I always gave my turn away. That's the kind of kid I was."

A core rule of life is that people become less grateful the longer they have it better.

"I got up at five o'clock in the morning—two hours after I was allowed to go to bed—and sewed up the holes in my one pair of pants. I split a cornflake for breakfast with my seven brothers, then I carried them all to school on my back. And I was grateful for what I had."

By comparison, what are our kids going to tell their kids? "Five hundred fifty channels. That's all we had when I was a boy. You had to make your sister find the remotes for you; we only had nine of them. All of the power buttons were up at the top. You had to stretch your thumb to get that far power button. Sometimes you hurt stuff in your wrist.

"I remember one winter got so bad that after my mother finished shoveling the driveway, she collapsed halfway up the walk. I had to step over her carrying my hot chocolate, and I almost tripped. I should have sued her."

In fact, most of our kids do have it better than most of us did—materially and "leisurely," that is. So what's a parent to do?

A second core law of life: If you have less, you appreciate it more. Thus, let's start by giving your daughter less. Start by reassessing what she has in perks, social freedoms, privileges and what she has to do to earn them. Some basic starting points:

1. Anything electronic in her room—TV, computer, video games, side-by-side refrigerator/freezer, six-line phone hookup—

consider removing, either to a family space or out of the house altogether. Technology is great, but it can easily come to dominate a child's idea of "the good life."

2. Give less allowance for more chores. The average kid probably earns about $16 per chore hour given the big money they get for little work. Forge a stronger link between money and cooperation. The cooperation must also be willing, not begrudging.

3. Link social freedoms not only to maturity level but also to cooperation. If your daughter wants to go to a friend's birthday party, before you give a *yes,* make her give a *yes* to some chores, cleaning, schoolwork and so on. In essence, social freedom and material goodies are not entitlements that come with age and breathing; they are privileges that have to be earned.

4. Pay close attention to her ongoing attitude. If it doesn't improve, that's a sign you may need to reassess what your daughter is getting for what she's giving. It's very easy to think we're pretty tight as parents when, in fact, a lot of looseness is flying underneath our radar.

Our culture is the wealthiest and most materially comfortable in the history of the world. Raising grateful kids takes a lot of effort. It doesn't come as naturally as it would if getting more came harder.

A Room With a View

Dear Dr. Ray,
   Do you think a teenager should have a television in his room?
                                                    Spouses Who Disagree

No. In print my response to your question looks quiet and calm. If you could hear my answer, it would sound something like *NOOO!!*

A mother once told me that her fourteen-year-old son was given a television by his grandmother. Mom abhorred the idea of a TV in her son's bedroom, mostly because of its moral—or lack thereof—content, but Grandma warned, "I gave it to him. It is now his, and if you take it out, you'll deal with me."

In an effort to sustain a shaky peace, Mom acquiesced. She asked me if I thought she had the right to take something someone had given her son.

I asked, "If a classmate gives your son a bag of marijuana, would you confiscate it?"

"Of course," she said.

"Why?"

"Because it is harmful to him."

I replied, "Then you've answered your own question. You have not only the right but the duty to protect your son from harmful influences, from wherever they come."

The fact that it was Grandma causing the problem complicated the picture, but Grandma boxed Mom into a corner with her gift's conditions, effectively forcing her to choose between her son and family strife. Grandma's attitude was, what does this harm? Sadly, so often in modern parenting that is the guiding question. And if a parent can't provide a compelling "harm," her stand may crumble, and she'll find herself yielding to the opinions of others, her children's desires or the flow of the culture's winds.

If you view parenting as the imparting of morals and character to children over the course of twenty or so years (in some cases, over the course of thirty or more), the question is not, what does this harm? The question is, what good does it impart?

Using the latter question, though we also could use the former to provide plenty of reasons to unplug your son's personal TV, let's make our case. In the area of morals, is standard TV fare in line with your values? Will it reinforce all you're trying to teach? Will it uplift your son's mind and spirit? Do the attitudes it promotes—toward faith, parents, authority, self-restraint, sex, family—fit well with your own?

If you've answered "yes" to these questions, then at least from a character perspective, television is your ally. Its unsupervised presence in your son's room will help to complete any areas of moral development your parenting may have missed. But I suspect your answers are more like mine: *NOOO!!*

Now let's consider family time. Will the television nudge your son closer to the family or pull him from it? If you're not sure, answer this question: is TV more entertaining than you are? Kids are attracted naturally to being entertained. Will your relationship with your son deepen if you're competing with thirty-seven channels and a remote?

Some parents qualify their TV placement with, "It doesn't have cable, and the reception isn't real good." I've often wondered if this was their best defense or their only.

How about activity? Does the availability of private viewing raise or lower the likelihood your son will read, do schoolwork, interact with siblings, do chores, lift weights, even converse with you? Will the room television option broaden your son's horizons or narrow them?

Sadly, if a teenager does not have a television in his room, he is now in the minority, an increasingly smaller one. Sadly, if parents do not allow the teen a TV, they too are in a dwindling minority. Gladly, they still can know they are right.

In making wise decisions regarding our children's welfare, we often need to answer many questions. And the answers may not lead us where much of society is headed. But they will serve to clarify just what may be the results of a particular decision.

There is no doubt in my mind that our fast-forward culture is making parenting an emotionally turbulent ride. Why allow things into your family that only will work against what you are working for?

Disciplining for Others

Dear Dr. Ray,

My son's religion teacher does not have good control of her class. My son, age thirteen, and several others boys act up. She has asked me to discipline him. I think it's her responsibility to maintain order, not mine.

Not There

It is and it isn't. (Don't you just love shrinks?)

If your son's teacher maintained better class discipline, your son most likely would behave better. However, it seems that her class structure is lacking, so you are being asked to provide discipline backup. You believe you shouldn't have to and wouldn't have to if she were better at this. Further, you're not at the scene of the trouble; she is. So she's better positioned to correct it. All of this you can legitimately argue until you run headlong into an overriding truth: It is her class, but he is your son.

Almost all humans will behave for those with the unassailable power to control them.

A friend told me of a situation similar to yours, except that the teacher made a more urgent demand. My friend's son would not be permitted back into class unless Mom came too and sat with him. My friend felt this was grossly unreasonable and asked my opinion.

I answered with a question (yet another chafing shrink tactic): "Susan, do you want your son to behave for and respect only those people who can control him?"

"Of course not," she said.

"Then you will have to teach him to respect all people, including those who aren't strong enough to teach him themselves."

Throughout a child's life he or she will encounter all types of discipline styles—some powerful, some pitiful. Grandparents, teachers, babysitters, neighbors, coaches, tutors: all will interact with a young-ster for better or for worse discipline-wise. Those who seldom have trouble with a child make a parent's discipline role that much easier. Those who can't or won't discipline will force the parent to carry their load. There is no way around this reality for the parent who wishes to raise a child who treats all people well, the tough and the soft.

Behaving even for weak disciplinarians is one sign of a well-devel-oping character (or perhaps a mild or cooperative temperament). Almost all humans—good character or not—will behave for those with the unassailable power to control them: police officers, drill ser-geants, judges. Most will cooperate with competent disciplinarians: a savvy teacher, demanding coach, confident sitter. Only those on their way to exemplary character will act well toward the pushovers. They have learned from their parents' discipline over the years to treat others well, no matter how strong or weak those others are.

Only those on their way to exemplary character will act well toward the pushovers.

So my opinion is that you need to inform your son in no uncertain terms that you will act immediately and definitely if you get even a whiff that he was disruptive for his religion teacher. You don't care if every other kid in the class is obnoxious. You will insure that he will be cooperative for her no matter how weakly she disciplines.

A Force for Good

Dear Dr. Ray,

What do you think about the idea that forcing adolescents to attend church against their will only breeds more resistance and eventually could deaden their faith altogether?

Making Them Anyway

I think it is clichéd, illogical, infinitely stupid and soul-jeopardizing. (We shrink types are trained to communicate our opinions in soft, affirming language.)

It is clichéd thinking. So many utterly shallow notions now dominate the parenting landscape, and for little reason other than that they are repeated endlessly and challenged seldom. They become mantras.

For instance, "Don't force a child to do anything he strongly opposes because he'll only rebel further." Better to negotiate, compromise or follow the child's lead, so that what you desire for him will gradually become his desire for him. Push too hard, so goes the warning, and he'll only push back harder. He won't come to accept personally your way of thinking or doing.

I don't think it's an overstatement to assert that for almost all of human history—except perhaps for the enlightened present—parents instinctively understood that if they wanted a child to embrace a way of life, they had to expose him to it, often against his will. They realized that he was not in a position to know better than a parent what was in his long-range good. Did all those people in all those times and places get it wrong, and we moderns finally figured out how kids really need to be guided?

The notion is illogical. If a child resists healthy food and seeks mainly candy and cupcakes, by mandating good nutrition, will you risk shaping her into a raging sugar addict who will someday regurgitate all your forced feeding? Similarly, suppose a youngster needs long-term medical treatment but struggles against it, becoming more frustrated with time. If you insist, and yes, force him to take his medicine, will he begrudgingly swallow it for now, persevering only until he is old enough to chuck it all? Or as he matures will he come to see the need, indeed the value, of what you made him do?

It is the nature of children—even adults—to initially fight what is of the most good to us.

Alas, it is the nature of children—even adults—to initially fight what is of the most good to us.

It is infinitely stupid and soul-jeopardizing. Nothing compares in importance to a child's infinite well-being. Everything is of no ultimate matter if it does not lead a person step-by-step closer to God. To allow a child to retreat from a relationship with the Almighty because he wants to, or because he's bored, or because he sees little present value in it or "because because" is to cooperate in a decision the results of which neither the child nor the parent can foresee. It is to allow a child to ignore and potentially to reject her very reason for existing.

Further, just being present in worship, however marginally, gives a chance for a homily to shape thoughts, for a prayer to soften a heart—in essence, for God's grace to work. Simply put, the risks of not visiting God far outweigh the risks of temporarily being forced to visit him.

OK, so it's to church whether a youngster wants to go or not. Then comes the critical part. We must be able to convey to our children why religion is of infinite worth: the logic, the meaning, the depth of it all. This means we must educate ourselves about it. We cannot give to our children what we ourselves don't possess. We must learn, know and understand the reasons why we worship as we do. As we give these to our children, their own understanding and their own commitment slowly will replace their resistance.

Index

A

activities
  balance of, 16–18
  commitments to, 105–107
  guidelines for weighing, 18
addenda, 80–81
adolescence
  balancing of activities during, 16–18
  behaviors during, historically, 2–3, 27
  physical development's influence on, 2
allowances
  ascertaining amounts for, 96, 97–99
  family chores v. wage chores and, 95–97
anger diffusion, 58–60
arguments. *See also* back talk; comebacks,
    teen; communication
  back talk's relation to, 74–75
  ending, 33–35
  guidelines for respect during, 29–30
  picking your battles concept and,
    146–148
  sibling, 91–95
attention-related misbehavior, 11–12
  ignoring, 13–14
authority-discipline
  anger diffusion in, 58–60
  changing teens' perceptions of, 52–54
  consistency in, 49–50
  discord between parents regarding, 67–70
  driving privileges as tool of, 54–55
  egalitarianism in parental roles of, 89–90
  house rules for, 69–70
  illusory, 65–67
  late starts in, 43–45

parental childhood overcompensation and,
    47–48
  reversal of direction in, 45–46, 49–50
  room confinement as tool of, 56–57
  testing of parental, 51–54
  time allotments for, 61–64, 65, 66–67, 83

B

back talk. *See also* arguments; comebacks,
    teen; communication
  grumbling as form of, 74–75
  nasty forms of, 75–77
  punishment tips regarding, 76
  respect's relation to, 29–30
battered parent syndrome, 71–73
behavioral contracts, 125–127. *See also*
    house rules
behavioral issues. *See also* authority-
    discipline; communication;
    respect; social freedom; strength and
    consistency, parental; trademarked
    troubles, teens
  attention-seeking related, 11–14
  authority-discipline connection to, 43–70,
    83, 89–90
  communicational, 19–42
  cultural v. developmental causes of, 2–3,
    14, 153
  entitlement as cause of, 2–3
  family v. nonfamily occurrence of, 3–4
  forced familial contact's relation to,
    14–16
  medical disorders as cause of, 9–11
  middle child syndrome, 7–9

168

motives for, 12
parental looks as deterrent to, 84–85
peer comparisons' relation to, 5–7
respect-oriented, 4–5, 29–30, 71–90, 135, 152–153
social freedom-related, 117–141, 150–151
strength and consistency approaches to, 5–7, 143–167
terminology used in describing, 51
trademarked teen, 91–115
blackout, 53–54
boredom
    activity overexposure's relation to, 18
    quality time's relation to, 26

C
cell phones, 130–133
chores
    allowances for, 95–97
    resistance to, 99–101
comebacks, teen, 83–85. *See also* arguments; back talk
communication
    argument avoidance in, 33–35
    lecturing as block to, 30–33
    listening's role in, 23–24, 27–29
    parents' adolescent misbehavior and, 41–42
    persistency's importance in, 37–39
    quality v. quantity of shared time and, 25–27
    reasonable expectations in relation to, 39–41
    reasoning limits within, 35–37
    respect's relevance to, 29–30
    strategies for parent-teen, 20–22, 29–30
    understanding of teen's relation to, 27–29
comparisons. *See also* specific comparisons
    parent-based, 103–105, 124, 143, 149–150, 150–151, 152–153, 154–156
    peer-based, 5–7, 132, 153–156
computer use, 139–141
consensus parenting. *See also* parent-based comparisons
    lowered standards-related, 143, 154–155
    social freedom-related, 124

consistency. *See also* strength and consistency, parental
    authority-discipline and, 49–50
    behavioral problems due to lack of, 5–7, 143–167
    communicational persistence and, 37–39
    maladjustment of teens and, 143–145
culture. *See also* social freedom
    cell phones' role in exposure to, 131
    development of teens influenced by, 9–11, 120, 128, 131–132, 150–151, 153, 162–163
    entitlement aspects of modern, 2–3
    forcing of familial contact's relation to, 14–16
    respect in contemporary, 152–153
    social freedom perceptions influenced by, 120–121
curfews
    breaking of, 137–139
    negotiation of, 135–137

D
dating, 128–130
development, teen
    behavioral expectations during, 153
    discipline's relation to, 143–146, 159, 166–167
    entitlement related to modern, 2–3
    separation-based aspects of, 14–16
    socialization related to, 9–11, 120, 128, 131–132, 150–151, 153, 162–163
    suggestions for positive, 3
discipline. *See also* authority-discipline
    addenda, forms of, 80–81
    attention-seeking misbehavior and, 11–14
    authority promotion's influence on, 43–70, 83, 89–90
    consistency in, 5–7, 49–50, 143–167
    criticism of, 151–153
    decline of contemporary, 151–153
    development, teen, related to, 143–146, 159, 166–167
    egalitarianism in parental, 89–90
    illusory, 65–67
    parental discord regarding, 67–70

parental looks as deterrent to, 84–85
persistence in, 61–67
reasoning's connection to, 37
relaxation of, 5–7
and responsibilities outside home,
164–165
school-related, 111–113
social freedom misconduct and, 121–123
socialization's relation to, 10–11,
120–121, 128, 132, 151, 153,
162–163
time allotment for results of, 61–64, 65,
66–67, 83
tips for effective, 62
traditional v. "enlightened" forms of,
56–57
double-jeopardy, disciplinary, 111–113
driving privileges
allowance of, 133–135
authority-discipline using, 54–55

E
entitlement, 2–3
essay writing
respect taught through, 81–83
suggested rules for, 82
expression, teen, 85–87

F
"five Ws," 117–119
force
familial contact by, 14–16
religious studies by, 165–167
friendships, teen, 127. *See also* peer-based
comparisons
dating, 128–130

G
gratitude
complaining's relation to, 159–161
teaching of, 158–159

H
house rules, 69–70. *See also* behavioral
contracts

L
lectures, 30–33. *See also* communication
listening, 23–24. *See also* communication
communicational accusations regarding,
27–29

M
maladjustment, teen, 143–146. *See also*
development, teen
MCS. See middle child syndrome (MCS)
medical disorders, 9–11
middle child syndrome (MCS), 7–9
mothers
authority perceptions and, 156–158
disciplinary egalitarianism and, 89–90

N
nagging
parental, 5, 65, 156–157
teen, 87–88
nonfamily. *See also* comparisons
double jeopardy discipline and, 111–113
and respect of authority figures, 152–153
school discipline and, 111–113, 164–165
teens' behavior with, 3–4

O
overcompensation, parental, 47–48
overprotection, parental, 150–151

P
parent-based comparisons
disciplinary compliance and, 152–153
overprotection and, 150–151
room cleanliness and, 103–105
standards, lowering of, and, 143,
149–150, 154–156
trust perceptions and, 124
parents. *See also* authority-discipline;
communication; respect; strength
and consistency, parental
adolescent histories of, 20, 41–42, 47–48,
160
authority-discipline tie to, 43–70, 83,
89–90
behavior's relation to facial expressions
of, 84–85

communication issues between teen and, 19–42

consensus parenting by, 124, 143, 154–155

disciplinary discord between, 67–70

egalitarianism in roles of, 89–90

expectations, reasonable, for, 39–41

familial contact forced by, 14–16

maladjustment related to mistakes of, 143–146

nagging by, 5, 65, 156–157

religious studies forced by, 165–167

respect's relation to, 4–5, 71–90

peer-based comparisons

cell phones and, 130–133

parental tips for confronting, 154–156

social freedom and, 5–7, 153–156

persistence

communicational, 37–39

disciplinary, 61–67

Q

quality time, 25, 27

boredom's relation to, 26

R

reasoning, 35–37

rebellion

due to over-strictness, 129, 148–150

religious-based, 165–167

religious studies, 165–167

respect, 88–89

addenda's relation to, 80–81

back talk as lack of, 74–77

battered parent syndrome and, 71–73

comebacks by teens as lack of, 83–85

communication's relevance to, 29–30

contemporary culture and, 152–153

development of, 4–5

driving privileges' relation to, 135

essay writing and lack of, 81–83

expressions of teens' relation to, 85–87

identification of teenagers' lack of, 71–73

nagging as lack of, 87–88

subtle forms of lack of, 77–79

rooms

keeping order in, 101–103

other parents' standards regarding, 103–105

sending kids to their, 56–57

televisions in kids', 161–163

S

school

disciplining for issues related to, 111–113

underachievement in, 107–111

shared time, 25–27

siblings

issues, physical, among, 91–93

issues, verbal, among, 93–95

smoking, 113–115

social freedom

age's relevance to, 119–121

bad peer influences and, 127–128

behavior contracts' use in relation to, 125–127

cell phone use by teens and, 130–133

computer use and, 139–141

curfew times in relation to, 135–139

dating and, 128–130

developmental relation to culture and, 9–11, 120, 128, 131–132, 150–151, 153, 162–163

driving's relation to, 133–135

"five Ws" related to, 117–119

overprotection fears and, 150–151

trust's relation to, 121–125

strength and consistency, parental. *See also* discipline

communicational persistence and, 37–39

comparisons to other families and, 153–156

discipline by others and, 164–165

discipline criticisms and, 151–153

discipline requirements for, 5–7

forced religious studies and, 165–167

grateful behavior taught through, 158–161

mothers' authority roles and, 156–158

overprotection fears and, 150–151

parental mistakes, maladjustment, and, 143–146

picking your battles and, 146–148
teen rebellion and, 129, 148–150,
    165–167
televisions in kids' rooms and, 161–163

T
television, 161–163
trademarked troubles, teens
    allowance disputes, 95–99
    chore resistance, 99–101
    commitment to activities, 105–107
    kids' room disorder, 101–105
    school and double-jeopardy discipline,
        111–113
    school-underachievement, 107–111
    sibling conflicts, physical, 91–93
    sibling conflicts, verbal, 93–95
    smoking, 113–115
trust
    discipline for breach of, 121–123
    teen perceptions regarding, 123–125

U
underachievement, school
    approaches for tackling, 108–111
    causes of, 107–108